HOT PROPERTY

A NEW COMEDY
IN TWO ACTS

By
FRED CARMICHAEL

AF893596

SAMUEL FRENCH, INC.
45 West 25th Street NEW YORK 10010
7623 Sunset Boulevard HOLLYWOOD 90046
LONDON TORONTO

Copyright ©, 1988, by Fred Carmichael

ALL RIGHTS RESERVED

CAUTION: Professionals and amateurs are hereby warned that HOT PROPERTY is subject to a royalty. It is fully protected under the copyright laws of the United States of America, the British Commonwealth, including Canada, and all other countries of the Copyright Union. All rights, including professional, amateur, motion pictures, recitation, lecturing, public reading, radio broadcasting, television, and the rights of translation into foreign languages are strictly reserved. In its present form the play is dedicated to the reading public only.

HOT PROPERTY may be given stage presentation by amateurs in theatres seating less than 500 upon payment of a royalty of Fifty Dollars for the first performance, and Thirty-five Dollars for each additional performance. PLEASE NOTE: for amateur productions in theatres seating over 500, write for special royalty quotation, giving details as to ticket price, number of performances and exact number of seats in your theatre. Royalties are payable one week before the opening performance of the play, to Samuel French, Inc., at 45 W. 25th St., New York, NY 10010; or at 7623 Sunset Blvd., Hollywood, CA 90046, or to Samuel French (Canada), Ltd., 80 Richmond St. East, Toronto, Ontario, Canada M5C 1P1.

Royalty of the required amount must be paid whether the play is presented for charity or gain and whether or not admission is charged.

Stock royalty quoted on application to Samuel French, Inc.

For all other rights than those stipulated above, apply to Samuel French, Inc.

Particular emphasis is laid on the question of amateur or professional readings, permission and terms for which must be secured in writing from Samuel French, Inc.

Copying from this book in whole or in part is strictly forbidden by law, and the right of performance is not transferable.

Whenever the play is produced the following notice must appear on all programs, printing and advertising for the play: "Produced by special arrangement with Samuel French, Inc."

Due authorship credit must be given on all programs, printing and advertising for the play.

Anyone presenting the play shall not commit or authorize any act or omission by which the copyright of the play or the right to copyright same may be impaired.

No changes shall be made in the play for the purpose of your production unless authorized in writing.

The publication of this play does not imply that it is necessarily available for performance by amateurs or professionals. Amateurs and professionals considering a production are strongly advised in their own interests to apply to Samuel French, Inc., for consent before starting rehearsals, advertising, or booking a theatre or hall.

No part of this book may be reproduced, stored in a retrieval system, or transmitted in any form, by any means, including mechanical, electronic, photocopying, recording, or otherwise, without the prior written permission of the publisher.

ISBN 0 573 66211 8

Printed in U.S.A.

IMPORTANT BILLING AND CREDIT REQUIREMENTS

All producers of HOT PROPERTY *must* give credit to the Author of the Play in all programs distributed in connection with performances of the Play and in all instances in which the title of the Play appears for purposes of advertising, publicizing or otherwise exploiting the Play and/or a production. The name of the Author *must* also appear on a separate line, in which no other name appears, immediately following the title, and *must* appear in size of type not less than fifty percent the size of the title type.

CAST

JAMIE DURWOOD
KAY MCNAUGHTON
ALBERTINE JOHNSON
MILLICENT TREVOR
SPENCER LEYTON
JOYCE INGALLS
H.L. BARRISTER
BUCK RANDALL

SCENE

The action of the play takes place in the combined office and living room of Jamie Durwood on the coast of California. The time is the present. Morning.

TIME

ACT ONE

SCENE 1
Morning of the present.

SCENE 2
Just before 8:00 P.M. that evening.

ACT TWO

Immediately following.

(The lights will dim to denote the passage of a few minutes.)

HOT PROPERTY

ACT I

Scene 1

SCENE: The action of the play takes place in the combined office-home of JAMIE DURWOOD on the California coast. It is a ranch style home and modern in design. The door to the outside is on the right wall with a small straight backed chair below it. Above the door and forming the corner of the room is a corner window looking out over the ocean. A window-seat is built-in below the window and to the L. along the upstage wall there are some tall plants. Up Center is an archway leading to the kitchen and the rest of the house with the exit to the L. A bulletin board is on the U.L. wall with newspaper clippings on it, etc. Another plant is in the corner. A desk is on the L. wall with a swivel chair in front of it and a typewriter table with typewriter below it. The desk faces a window which is open at the moment and foliage can be seen outside. Architectural drawings can be seen above the typewriter and the bulletin board. A phone is on the upstage of the desk and various papers and desk equipment is on the desk. A sofa is center stage with a small table to the R. of it and next to that an easy chair which is not too overstuffed but still comfortable. The overall effect is bright and sunny and modern. It is a morning of the present day.

AT RISE: JAMIE is seen pacing above the desk talking on the phone. JAMIE is probably in his thirties and is a pleasant-looking but harried man. He is dressed casually and slightly unkempt.

JAMIE. ... I can't understand it. I know I mailed that check last week ... Yes, I was a bit late but what with one thing and another and ... Yes, another check right away ... *(Looks about desperately for an idea to explain his actions.)* Why, look at that. I don't believe it. *(Covers phone.)* I hope you do. *(Into phone.)* Guess what's there? Right here behind my indoor dwarf banana tree ... You are right! Your check. That damned cat must have knocked it there ... Yes, I'll drive it right down to the post office now in my car, or rather your car. *(Gives a lame laugh.)* Thank you so much. *(Hangs up and sinks in swivel chair.)* Now I'll have to get a cat. I can't afford to feed one.

(Phone RINGS.)

JAMIE. Oh, damn. *(Speaks into it in falsetto voice.)* Durwood Enterprises, good morning. ... yes, sir ... I'm afraid Mr. Durwood has stepped out of the office for a moment. I'll have him call when he returns ... John Stoughton, yes, from the phone company ... yes, I'm writing it down. *(He isn't.)* Why, thank you. ... Yes, I have been told I have a sexy voice ... Tonight? Dinner? ... How delightful. I'm through my pre-natal Lamaze class at eight-thirty ... Hello, hello... *(Hangs up.)* Coffee! It must be ready by now.

(Starts for U.C. Exit when phone RINGS again. He answers in a dead monotone.)

JAMIE. This is Durwood Enterprises. This is a recording. No one is in the office the moment. They are all giving quarts at the blood bank... Leave a message when you hear the beep.

(Looks for a beep and moves typewriter carriage till it RINGS. Hangs up and again goes U.C. but this time there is a KNOCK on the front door.)

JAMIE. Not another. *(Goes to door and calls through it.)* Go away. Gas is escaping. There's a leak. *(coughs)* I'm the gas man.

KAY. *(outside door)* If you're the gas man then you've come to shut it off. The bill hasn't been paid in three months.

JAMIE. Kay, it's you. You're late. It's after ten.

KAY.*(OS)* You fired me three days ago.

JAMIE. Then go away. I can't even pay you minimum wage.

KAY. *(OS)* Open up. It's your birthday.

JAMIE. Are you bearing gifts?

KAY. *(OS)* You bet I am.

(JAMIE opens door and KAY MCNAUGHTON is there, She is a pretty girl in her twenties with a bright, refreshing attitude about life. She is dressed casually.)

JAMIE. You don't look like a Trojan horse.

KAY. *(Kisses him lightly and crosses below him to sofa.)* Happy birthday darling.

JAMIE. *(Closes door.)* You are the only nice thing that's happened to me all day. Every last person I owe money to has called. I'm about to become a statistic. *(Goes to her.)*

If there are three hundred thousand homeless in the U.S., it is about to become three hundred thousand and one.

KAY. Things are bound to get better.

JAMIE. That's what Caesar said on the Ides of March.

KAY. Oh, we are in a humorous mood this morning. Is the coffee made?

JAMIE. Mr. Coffee has been gargling away for minutes.

KAY. You sit there and await your present. I'll get the coffee. *(Exits U.C.)*

JAMIE. *(Sits on sofa.)* What I need is one of those cyanide pills so I can bite down on it in the lobby of the bank.

KAY. *(Off stage)* What you'll get is delicious coffee. It's mountain-grown.

JAMIE. All coffee is mountain-grown. Did you ever hear a TV commercial where they said, "These coffee beans are handpicked by Waldo Wilkins in the valleys of Appalachia?"

KAY. *(Enters with two cups of coffee.)* You're turning into a cranky old man. *(Hands him the cup and kisses him again.)* Happy birthday again.

JAMIE. I want my present.

JAMIE. Here it is.

JAMIE. Where?

KAY. Here. Me.

JAMIE. You?

KAY. I am giving you me. Surprise. I will marry you.

JAMIE. Surprise, I didn't ask you.

KAY. Surprise, you will.

JAMIE. I can't.

KAY. *(Sits beside him.)* Why not? Do you have an insane wife locked away in the attic, like Rochester?

JAMIE. That's in upstate New York.

KAY. That's in Jane Eyre and don't avoid the subject.

JAMIE. I'm not going to drag you down to my poverty level. You don't know the sort of Grapes my Wrath has.

KAY. I'm very capable of making a living. I'm a good secretary, aren't I?

JAMIE. You were fired three days ago.

KAY. Only because my boss couldn't pay me.

JAMIE. You go off and marry some rich old man, then murder him, come back to me with the inheritance and then we'll talk.

KAY. I will marry no one but you.

JAMIE. Do you mind waiting till I'm on Social Security?

KAY. Stop making cracks. I'm serious.

JAMIE. *(Rises and puts cup on table by sofa.)* So am I. My business is on the brink of complete collapse. I am sitting on the financial San Andreas Fault and you want to marry me.

KAY. I know prospects don't look good but—

JAMIE. My prospects make Chekhov look like Neil Simon. *(Crosses to window U.R.)* Look out there. That land on the ridge overlooking the Pacific Ocean is spectacular. It's for enjoying. It's for being outside your living room window, everyone's living room window. It's criminal putting a shopping center there.

KAY. *(Rises, puts her cup on desk and goes to him.)* I know how good your plans are.

JAMIE. Good? They're magnificent. *(Looks out window down the coast.)* Homes, not just for the rich and famous but for everyone, inexpensive and expensive all clustered together and with that view. *(Sinks down on window seat.)* God, I almost had it. If that damned storm hadn't blown in when it did—

KAY. Maybe Leyton will give you more time.

JAMIE. That is the stupidest statement I have ever heard.

KAY. Sorry.

JAMIE. Spencer Leyton has been trying to get hold of that land since before you came to work for me.

KAY. *(Sits by him.)* I know that.

JAMIE. He'll have it so crowded Pizza Hut will be on top of Burger King with Dunkin' Donuts in the basement.

KAY. Maybe if you appeal to him once more.

JAMIE. *(As if talking to a child, he gets his cup from table and crosses below the chair.)* Kay, darling, let me explain the facts of life.

KAY. *(Goes to him.)* Mommy already did that.

JAMIE. *(Sits in chair R. of sofa.)* I speak of business life. Spencer Leyton will stop at nothing to foreclose on me and get that land. The only income I've got left is some small royalties from Mother's books. And every time I see another ad for the new one, I could commit murder.

KAY. *(Goes to desk and drinks her coffee.)* There must be some way to prove your mother wrote, *"Inez."*

JAMIE. How?

KAY. Spencer Leyton couldn't have written it. He's no author. He builds shopping malls.

JAMIE. He's had articles published in technical magazines but nothing important. Then he sends Mother's original copy of *"Inez"* to H.L. Barrister, the publisher, with his name on it.

KAY. *(Crosses and sits on sofa.)* He put Willis Waxman's name ot it.

JAMIE. I don't care if he put Oliver Goldsmith on it, I knew Mother had written *"Inez."* Besides, Spencer has always used Willis Waxman as a pen name for those articles.

KAY. And *"Inez"* is going to make a fortune.

JAMIE. *(Puts his cup down and goes to desk for newspaper which is folded open.)* Did you see the *L.A. Times* yesterday?

KAY. I never got past Dear Abby.

JAMIE. *(Crosses to her with paper.)* Right in here another ad and another good review.

KAY. I wish I'd known your mother. I read one of her other books, *"Return of Love."* but it wasn't as sexy as I gather *"Inez"* is. They say it's required reading for Masters and Johnson.

JAMIE. Was I surprised. Mother told me she was going to write a best-seller no matter how far her standards had to plummet. Listen *(reads)* "Move over Jackie Collins, stand aside Harold Robbins, Willis Waxman has arrived on the sexy scene. The book is *"Inez"* and she makes

"Lolita" look like Grandma Moses. This is summer reading at its most provocative. Turn down the hot tubs, turn up the air conditioners and read *"Inez."* It goes on and on like that.

KAY. *(Has noticed what is on back page of what he has been reading.)* Look at that!

JAMIE. What?

KAY. *(Puts her cup on table and takes paper. Reads.)* "Fire at Sequoia Playhouse closes season."

JAMIE. *(Sits on sofa.)* Anyone hurt?

KAY. No, but the theatre's out for the rest of the season. Poor Albertine.

JAMIE. Who?

KAY. Albertine Johnson. She and Mother went to school together back in Muncie. She's an actress.

JAMIE. I never heard of her.

KAY. *(as she reads article)* She seems to keep working quietly but non-stop. We exchange Christmas cards and occasionally she sends a program from somewhere. This was a summer tour booked into the Sequoia Playhouse for a week and then going on.

JAMIE. We all got troubles. I am being foreclosed and she is already foreclosed.

KAY. You shouldn't have given Spencer a mortgage on that development.

JAMIE. *(Takes paper back to desk.)* Oh, hindsight is great. *(Leans back on desk.)* I never thought he looked on me as a rival in the development business but he must have. Anyway, when he offered me the loan at a lower percentage than the bank I grabbed it.

KAY. And your mother really liked him?

JAMIE. I thought so. She was always willing to help aspiring authors. I suppose Spencer was using her, she was such an innocent.

(KNOCK on front door.)

KAY. *(rises)* Who's that?

JAMIE. How do I know? Electric company? Diner's Club? Girl Scout cookies? I owe everyone.

(KNOCK again.)

KAY. *(Puts cup on table and goes to door.)* I'd better go and see.

JAMIE. Open at your own risk.

(KAY opens door and ALBERTINE JOHNSON is there. She is definitely a character actress as she is probably in her sixties but has a very youthful spirit and outlook on life. Being an actress she tends to the theatrical but there is a wonderfully warm, grandmotherly side to her. She is a fun person to be with.)

KAY. Yes?

ALBERTINE. Your doorbell is broken.

KAY. I know.

ALBERTINE. Is this Kay McNaughton? Kay, dear, is this you?

KAY. I hope so.

ALBERTINE. You've changed your hair. You've changed your height. You've changed your weight. It's been too many years.

KAY. *(Thinks a moment.)* Albertine Johnson, it is you.

ALBERTINE. *(as they embrace)* In the sagging flesh.

KAY. We were just talking about you. The fire. You're unemployed.

ALBERTINE. *(Comes in and KAY closes the door.)* Just for the week, dear. We're booked into the Palm Acres Theatre next Tuesday.

KAY. You're all right? You weren't burnt or anything?

ALBERTINE. Some apprentice left the electric glue pot on all night. Either that or the producer did it. We didn't get exactly money reviews. *(Sees JAMIE and crosses in C.)* You must be Durwood of the Enterprises.

JAMIE. *(Goes to her.)* You hit it.

ALBERTINE. I saw the sign out front.

KAY. Albertine Johnson, this is Jamie Durwood.

ALBERTINE. *(as they shake)* So nice to meet you.

KAY. She's the actress.

JAMIE. Of course. *(Crosses to desk.)* I knew you looked familiar.

ALBERTINE. Don't be silly. You neither recognize me nor have ever heard of me. I'm no star. I'm a "never was." Some are has beens but I never was. I always worked though, and it's been a wonderful life. *(laughs)* Oh, dear, I sound like Jimmy Stewart in the movie of the same name. I wish they'd never colorized it, don't you?

KAY. Sit down, Albertine, let me get you some coffee. *(ALBERTINE sits on sofa as KAY goes to archway.)* How did you find me here? *(Exits.)*

ALBERTINE. Just black dear, thanks. Well, after the fire, we seem to have this week off so the cast all got together and came down here for a well-earned vacation. We're at the Pebble Manor Hotel. It's very nice right there on the beach.

KAY. *(Off stage)* It's lovely.

ALBERTINE. So I popped round to your address and your neighbor, the one with the barking dachshund and the dyed blonde hair—

KAY. *(Off stage)* Mrs. Klemmer.

ALBERTINE. That's the one. She told me you were probably here, you'd been fired but you were probably working anyway. *(As KAY Enters with coffee. To JAIME.)* What's the matter, don't you pay her?

JAMIE. To be brutally frank, no.

ALBERTINE. *(Takes coffee.)* Is it true you work for nothing?

KAY. For the time being. *(Goes to JAMIE and puts her arm around him.)* Jamie here is my fiancé.

JAMIE. No, I'm not.

KAY. Yes, he is.

ALBERTINE. If he doesn't pay you to work for him he'd better be your fiancé.

KAY. It's under discussion at the moment.

ALBERTINE. When I played ingenues I always married the young man at the final curtain — if it was a comedy.

JAMIE. *(Goes below KAY to C.)* This is pure Greek tragedy, *"Medea Meets Godzilla."*

ALBERTINE. Nonsense. this is a bright, cheery room just made for comedy. Nothing bad can happen here.

JAMIE. *(Goes to window U.R.)* It's about to.

ALBERTINE. What's the matter with you two? Young

love take a tragic turn.?

KAY. It's this way—

JAMIE. *(Sinks on window seat.)* No, Kay, don't bother her with our problems when the theatre's just been burnt out from under her.

ALBERTINE. *(Cup on table and goes to him.)* That's nothing. I'm used to closing out of town. Anyway, I reopen next week. Now, what is wrong?

KAY. Did you notice that gorgeous strip of land right down there? *(points)*

ALBERTINE. You mean where the foundations are all in?

KAY. That's the one. It's a Durwood Enterprises project.

ALBERTINE. And you're that very Durwood?

JAMIE. That same lucky man.

KAY. *(Crosses to them.)* It's going to be an apartment complex with homes for all income levels. It's a pet project of Jamie's.

JAMIE. *(rises)* But the last storm did some damage. I'm out of money, the foreclosure is imminent and it's going to become a shopping mall. Curtain. Applause. *(Gets his cup from table and goes to the desk.)*

ALBERTINE. You can't borrow any more money?

JAMIE. Not a sou.

KAY. And it's all criminal, illegal.

ALBERTINE. What is?

KAY. Jamie is due a fortune from his mother.

ALBERTINE. An inheritance?

JAMIE. *(Sits in swivel chair and turns it to window.)* Let's just skip it, huh?

ALBERTINE. *(Goes to him.)* After that morose prologue, I need to know the whole plot.

KAY. To begin with, do you know who Jamie's mother was?

ALBERTINE. Other than Mrs. Durwood, no.

KAY. Does the name Doris Durwood strike a bell?

ALBERTINE. Doris? Of course, the authoress. All those nice books one could send one's maiden aunt for Christmas.

KAY. Not the latest one.

ALBERTINE. Which is that? *(Laughs as she picks up her cup and sits in chair right.)* I'm always reading backstage. We pass books around the company and last week I missed an entrance reading one. On stage they kept ad-libbing "Here she comes." "I know she'll be here soon" and other thrillers like that. I finally realized it and left Inez seducing a Russian commissar.

KAY and JAMIE. Inez?

ALBERTINE. Yes, the book. *"Inez."* You must have heard of it.

JAMIE. That's Mother's book.

ALBERTINE. No, it's by a — someone else. No one ever remembers authors unless it's Shakespeare.

KAY. *(Goes below sofa.)* Jamie's mother wrote *"Inez."*

JAMIE. *(rises)* I know it says Willis Waxman, but—

ALBERTINE. That's the name, Willis Waxman.

JAMIE. There is no such person.

ALBERTINE. It's your mother's nom de plume?

JAMIE. The book was stolen from her.

ALBERTINE. Impossible. I've been on loads of those TV caper movies, everything from bank heists to the crown jewels, but no one ever steals a book.

KAY. But Spencer Leyton did.

ALBERTINE. Who's he?

KAY. Willis Waxman.

ALBERTINE. You're both dear people and I have spent my life acting in plays with mistaken identity, but you are outdoing Moliere. Who is who?

KAY. *(Sits on sofa.)* Spencer Leyton stole Doris Durwood's book and it's published under the name of Willis Waxman.

ALBERTINE. What Feydeau could do with this. Just give me a one, two, three explanation, please.

JAMIE. *(Crosses above sofa.)* We must start with my one ambition and that is to have my development down there on the coast, a place with living quarters for all sizes of income.

ALBERTINE. I see, dear. You're the one with the white hat.

JAMIE. That what?

ALBERTINE. The white hat. The hero. Now who wears the black hat?

KAY. Spencer Leyton.

JAMIE. He's built all those shopping malls up and down the coast.

ALBERTINE. He's a big rival then?

JAMIE. Not until now. *(Circles to the right of her.)* I'm just a beginner, but he wanted that land and I got it first.

ALBERTINE. Ah, the conflict is looming. Good. Go on. Into act two.

JAMIE. When I needed money, suddenly a mortgage became available at below bank rates.

ALBERTINE. Through Spencer?

JAMIE. You got it.

ALBERTINE. No, you got it. Go on, the tension is building.

JAMIE. You have to understand that Spencer is a frustrated writer.

KAY. He's had some technical articles published in unknown magazines and two novels.

ALBERTINE. That's hardly frustrated.

JAMIE. Vanity publications.

ALBERTINE. Where you pay all the expenses yourself?

KAY. And he published them under the name Willis Waxman so no one will know he pays to have them published.

ALBERTINE. I agree with Katharine Hepburn who says she never puts money in her own plays.

JAMIE. *(Moves above sofa.)* So suddenly Mother starts going to Spencer's office all the time. I found he'd underwritten the loan if she promised to write her next book up there with him watching her create. She said he was going to write a book on how to write a book.

ALBERTINE. Make a nice Christmas present for James Michener.

JAMIE. But Mother told me his writing was secondary. His primary thrust was to get my land. That's when *"Inez"* was born.

ALBERTINE. The idea for the book?

JAMIE. *(Crosses and sits on sofa.)* Mother said she'd better write a best-seller and get it published before my loan came due. She said she'd follow the pattern and write the exploits of a woman of mystery, namely Inez.

ALBERTINE. She hit it, mystery and sex.

JAMIE. She said I'd blush to read it as I didn't think she knew all those kinky things but the royalties would ensure the development being finished. She was quite a woman.

ALBERTINE. Somewhere between Joan of Arc and Sadie Thompson.

KAY. Then that storm came.

JAMIE. The one last October.

KAY. Repairing the damage to the foundations put us way behind schedule.

JAMIE. Mother died just a year ago and I—

ALBERTINE. Spencer murdered her!

KAY. Albertine!

JAMIE. Of course not.

ALBERTINE. Sorry, it's all those British mysteries I've been in. And I'm usually the one who is murdered and I have to spend act two crocheting in my dressing room.

JAMIE. After she died, I went to Spencer to gather her writings. He said there weren't any, just a few notes and he had thrown them out. I knew there was *"Inez"* but he said it hadn't worked out and she had torn it up.

KAY. *(Picks up her cup from table and JAMIE'S from desk.)* Then the book comes out with Willis Waxman's name on it and the foreclosure on the loan comes in.

JAMIE. And I can't touch the royalties, Mother's inheritance.

ALBERTINE. And Hamlet thought things were rotten in Denmark.

KAY. There's no way Jamie can prove it's Doris' book. *(Exits to the kitchen with the cups.)*

JAMIE. *(Rises and moves D.R.)* I wrote the publisher, H.L. Barrister, and got a nice form letter back saying people always claim they wrote a novel when it is headed for the best-seller lists.

ALBERTINE. Inez is a fascinating character. She must have seen more mattresses than Mr. Beautyrest, whoever he is.

JAMIE. *(Sinks in chair D.R.)* There's nothing like meeting a stranger and immediately telling her your woes.

ALBERTINE. You "depend on the kindness of strangers." Tennessee Williams said that. Now, what's going to happen? You can't let it stop here.

JAMIE. I've done everything I can think of.

ALBERTINE. Something will happen. At this point, when I'm in a play, suddenly the doorbell rings.

JAMIE. It's broken.

ALBERTINE. That's right. Then suddenly there is a knock on the door.

(There is a KNOCK on the front door.)

ALBERTINE. You see?

(KAY Enters.)

JAMIE. *(whispers)* If we're quiet that bill collector might evaporate. *(Crosses by door listening.)*

KAY. You've got to face them sooner or later.

JAMIE. Later.

ALBERTINE. It might be Publishers Clearing House with a ten million dollar prize.

JAMIE. I'll open it.

ALBERTINE. Besides, it gives drama to the situation.

(JAMIE opens the door and MILLICENT TREVOR is there. She is a sophisticated forty and smartly dressed. Ususally, she appears very cool and collected but with a bubbling sense of humor. At the moment she is desperately frazzled.)

JAMIE. Yes, I—

MILLICENT. *(Rushes in, closing door, and leans against it. Breathless.)* Close the door. Quick.

JAMIE. What's the matter?

KAY. We don't know you, do we?

ALBERTINE. She could be serving a subpoena.

MILLICENT. Please, don't give me away.

JAMIE. To whom?

MILLICENT. He's out there. He's after me.

JAMIE. Who?

MILLICENT. Him! *(Opens door, and peeks out, slams it again.)* He's still there. He's got a gun.

KAY. *(Goes to phone on desk.)* Call the police!

MILLICENT. He is the police.

JAMIE. Constable Wilkins is after you?

MILLICENT. Your Wilkins is trying to stop me from getting to the CIA before I — before I—

KAY. Before you what?

MILLICENT. Die! *(Collapses in JAMIE'S arms so her head is upside down facing C.)* I've been poisoned. I can't hold out much longer.

JAMIE. Don't die here.

ALBERTINE. *(rises)* Do you have a stomach pump?

MILLICENT. You! *(Rises and crosses to ALBERTINE.)* How did you get here?

ALBERTINE. I'm a friend of the family.

MILLICENT. *(Turns to JAMIE desperately.)* Don't you know who she is?

KAY. Albertine Johnson.

MILLICENT. No, no, she's the mole in the CIA, she's the spy. It is she who poisoned me. *(With a gasp she falls to the floor.)*

JAMIE. Oh, my God!

KAY. *(Crosses in.)* What'll we do. Is she dead?

ALBERTINE. *(calmly)* You really believed all that? I thought it was overacting.

MILLICENT. *(Opens her eyes and sits up on the floor.)* I was underplaying.

JAMIE. She's alive!

ALBERTINE. Compared to what you do at the opening of act two, I admit that was underplaying.

MILLICENT. *(as ALBERTINE helps her up)* And what's the matter with what I do at the opening of act two?

ALBERTINE. *(smiles)* I'm only kidding. You're so sensitive.

KAY. What is going on?

MILLICENT. Your doorbell is broken.

JAMIE. I know.

MILLICENT. It almost ruined my entrance.

ALBERTINE. Permit me to introduce our resident "other woman." This is Millicent Trevor. Millie, this is my friend Kay McNaughton and her possible fiancé

Jamie Durwood.

MILLICENT. Delighted to meet people who support me so beautifully.

JAMIE. You were just putting on an act?

ALBERTINE. We call it an improv.

MILLICENT. Improvisation.

ALBERTINE. One of us starts acting and the other picks it up. You were very good, Millie.

MILLICENT. I liked your line about the stomach pump.

ALBERTINE. Just be glad they don't have one.

MILLICENT. *(Crosses below her to KAY.)* Should I apologize or did you have a good time?

KAY. *(Sits in desk chair.)* It was a little startling, I admit. Do you do this often?

MILLICENT. Heavens, no. Just once in awhile to keep our talents honed.

JAMIE. You were very convincing.

MILLICENT. Oh, dear. "Very convincing" isn't a good review. It's like "quite adequate." Couldn't you say "thoroughly dynamic, powerful throughout" or something like that?

KAY. "Compelling." How's that?

MILLICENT. Excellent. *(to ALBERTINE:)* I like these two.

ALBERTINE. *(Sits on sofa.)* And wait till you find out what Jamie's mother did.

MILLICENT. I blush to think.

ALBERTINE. She wrote *"Inez."*

MILLICENT. The book?

ALBERTINE. Yes.

MILLICENT. You kid?

ALBERTINE. I don't.

MILLICENT. *(Goes to JAMIE.)* Your mother actually wrote that?

JAMIE. I'm afraid so.

MILLICENT. Does she have an asbestos word processor?

JAMIE. *(Moves D.R.)* Hardly.

MILLICENT. If you're her boy, then you must be the bastard son of that deposed count — what was his name?

JAMIE. It's not a real biography. It's just a novel.

MILLICENT. I keep thinking it's real, she writes so well. No, he — it's a man. Willis Waxman. He wrote it.

JAMIE. That's rather a long story.

MILLICENT. Your mother's pen name?

JAMIE. More or less.

ALBERTINE. Mostly less. It's a depressing story, Millie, and I shall tell it to you in great detail in a voice barely holding back the tears.

MILLICENT. *(Goes to her.)* We'd all be better off if you held them back a bit more on stage.

ALBERTINE. Well, really!

MILLICENT. *(Smiles as she sits in the chair.)* That makes us even for you saying I overacted.

ALBERTINE. Agreed. We're very good friends actually. We've acted together a number of times. I'm usually the maiden aunt and Millie here is either the murderess or the husband stealer.

MILLICENT. I've always been cast that way since kindergarten. Everyone else was a daisy or a tulip and what was I? Poison ivy.

ALBERTINE. But it makes a good living.

KAY. *(Rises and goes C.)* I've seen you on a commercial, haven't I?

ALBERTINE. Several, I hope.

KAY. You're a spy on a train. Yes, you wear that black hat with the feathers that come down over some of your face—

MILLICENT. All of my face until I found a pair of scissors.

KAY. And you steal the peppermints from the foreign agent and we see you eating them as the train pulls out and he's left on the platform peppermintless.

MILLICENT. I ate four dozen of those damn things that day and had to go on Weight Watchers.

KAY. *(Sits next to ALBERTINE on the sofa.)* You were so effective, I've been eating them ever since.

MILLICENT. I'm doing another in the fall when they add calcium.

JAMIE. How did you come to find Albertine here?

MILLICENT. She left me sitting out there in that rented Toyota.

ALBERTINE. My God, that's right. Oh, Millie, sorry. *(to the others:)* I told her to wait there and I'd see if this was the right place and then I got so fascinated with your story — *(Rises and goes to MILLICENT.)* oh, Millie, wait till you hear about *"Inez"* and the development and the book thief and, oh, it's better than *"The Cherry Orchard."*

MILLICENT. I hope it has more laughs.

KAY. It doesn't.

MILLICENT. I can't wait.

(KNOCK on the door.)

ALBERTINE. You may have to.

JAMIE. *(He and KAY rise.)* Perhaps it's another actor from your company.

KAY. Pretending to be Jimmy Hoffa.

MILLICENT. They're all down on the beach getting burnt.

(KNOCK on door again.)

SPENCER. *(Off stage)* Open up!

JAMIE. Now he's here, Simon Legree in person.

SPENCER. *(Off stage)* Your bell is broken.

JAMIE. If anyone else says that I shall put up a Chinese gong.

SPENCER. *(Off stage)* I know you're in there. I see your car hasn't been reclaimed yet.

KAY. *(to ALBERTINE:)* It's Spencer.

ALBERTINE. Spencer Leyton with the black hat?

KAY. You got it.

MILLICENT. *(rises)* I'm missing something.

ALBERTINE. You're missing everything.

JAMIE. *(Goes to door.)* I'll have to let him in.

SPENCER. *(Off stage)* You're damned right you will.

KAY. *(Guides her towards kitchen.)* Why don't you take Millicent into the kitchen and give her some coffee and gossip.

ALBERTINE. You mean tell her everything?

KAY. Yes.

SPENCER. *(Off stage)* I shall count to three. One—

KAY. Hurry.

ALBERTINE. Come on, Millie. *(MILLICENT goes to kitchen.)* I shall tell this so dramatically.

SPENCER. *(Off stage)* Two—

MILLICENT. *(as they Exit)* I'd love to see you audition for a mute.

SPENCER. *(Off stage)* Three.

KAY. *(Comes down.)* Open the door.

JAMIE. I always wonder what people do after "three."

SPENCER. *(Off stage)* I said, "Three."

JAMIE. They repeat.

(JAMIE opens door and SPENCER LEYTON is there. He is middle-aged, aggressive, and determined. He is dressed expensively but perhaps a bit flashy.)

SPENCER. I was only going to say "Three" one more time.

JAMIE. It isn't Monday yet so you can't have your money.

SPENCER. *(Crosses below him into the room.)* It isn't Monday yet and you don't have my money anyway.

KAY. But he will have it.

SPENCER. Well, Kay McNaughton. Rumor has it you were fired yet here you are. Doing some sort of charity work?

KAY. I am still working here, Mr. Leyton.

SPENCER. Then why don't you go type somewhere. I want to talk to Jamie.

KAY. *(Crosses to it.)* My typewriter is over here.

JAMIE. *(Moves below SPENCER to D.C.)* Perhaps you'd

better go, Kay. Take care of those odd things we have in the kitchen.

KAY. *(Goes to kitchen.)* Yes, of course. Odd, but very nice. *(Exits.)*

JAMIE. *(Coldly, turns to SPENCER.)* Now, Spencer, exactly what is it you want?

SPENCER. *(Puts arm on JAMIE'S shoulder which he promptly pushes off.)* Now, Jamie, boy, we don't want any unpleasantness, do we?

JAMIE. It's a little late for "we" to think of that, isn't it?

SPENCER. Come, come, let's talk this out. Aren't you going to offer me a morning coffee?

JAMIE. No.

SPENCER. I see.

JAMIE. I'm not going to offer you anything, *(Moves to windows D.R.)* especially not the Durwood Development down there.

SPENCER. *(Goes to him.)* I hate to foreclose on you, Jamie, you know that—

JAMIE. No, I don't know that.

SPENCER. But after all, it's the American way. Capitalism, we have to think of our business first, and my business is to see a shopper's paradise down there.

JAMIE. It's a paradise without the shops. Why spoil it?

(KAY Enters very agitated.)

KAY. I hate to interrupt—

SPENCER. Then don't.

JAMIE. What is it, Kay?

KAY. *(Comes D.C.)* I've lost those two odd things in the kitchen.

SPENCER. Can't you cook lunch after we're finished?

JAMIE. Then hurry up and finish. *(to KAY:)* I'm sure they're about somewhere. *(KAY opens front door and looks out.)*

SPENCER. Now, Jamie, the shopping mall will make a fortune and some of it can be yours.

JAMIE. No way.

(ALBERTINE'S and MILLICENT'S heads appear outside the open window L. and they listen. SPENCER does not see them.)

SPENCER. You're never going to raise the money by Monday, you know that, so why not give in now and join me? What say, no hard feelings? *(Extends his hand.)*

JAMIE. You're incredible, Spencer. You can't stand the thought that, even after you forclose on me and the development is yours, I'll keep fighting. You can't stand bad publicity.

KAY. *(Turns closing the door and sees the two outside the window. She signals to JAMIE.)* Oh!

SPENCER. *(to her:)* Now what?

JAMIE. Yes, Kay.

KAY. *(Backs out to kitchen awkwardly.)* I just remembered those odd things are outside. I'll go bring them in.

SPENCER. She used to be such a level-headed girl.

JAMIE. She still is.

SPENCER. *(Moves D.C.)* As far as business goes, I had

hoped we could come to some understanding...

JAMIE. I'm understanding plenty.

SPENCER. ...because of your dear mother.

JAMIE. *(Getting angry, moves D.R. of chair.)* Oh, now, let's not start on that.

SPENCER. I was terribly fond of Doris.

JAMIE. How can you say that when you've stolen her book? She wrote *"Inez"* and why don't you admit it?

SPENCER. What? Are you wired? Have you got this place bugged? *(Picks up small desk lamp.)* Is there a listening device under the lampshade?

JAMIE. *(Goes D.C.)* Don't be melodramatic. I know I got a cheap loan from you because of Mother's bargain.

SPENCER. I deny knowledge of any bargain.

JAMIE. If she hadn't had that heart attack all you'd have had was your piece on how she wrote a book.

SPENCER. It would have been published in *Writer's Digest* no doubt.

JAMIE. But instead you get ahold of a potential best-seller.

SPENCER. *(Goes to him.)* At the moment, Willis Waxman is the author of *"Inez."* All I will say, *(Raises his voice.)* in case there is a tape machine playing somewhere, is that if you decide to come along with me on the shopping mall I wouldn't be surprised if Willis Waxman didn't give you the rights to *"Inez."*

JAMIE. Is this bribery?

SPENCER. *(Goes below him to D.C.)* Call if charity.

JAMIE. You mean you'll give me what is rightfully mine and I won't spread the truth around about you?

SPENCER. *(Sits in the chair.)* All I have to do is write H.L.

Barrister, the publisher. He is aware that Willis Waxman is me. The royalties will be yours.

JAMIE. I've written H.L. Barrister and got a very courteous reply.

SPENCER. I know. I got a carbon copy. Barrister did admit that the style of the writing, although spicier, shall we say, was a good deal like Doris Durwood's but then I said I'd been working with her.

JAMIE. If only Mother had left some notes here, some drafts, something.

SPENCER. Doris was a dear lady and she certainly stuck to her bargain about *"Inez."*

JAMIE. Spencer, I will give you one concession.

SPENCER. Good, what is it?

JAMIE. *(Moves into him.)* I will let you escape from here without a bloody nose if you will go before I count to three, and I'll only say three once. One.

SPENCER. *(rises)* You wouldn't?

JAMIE. *(Moves in closer.)* Oh, wouldn't I? Two.

SPENCER. *(Backs up and opens door.)* I'll have you arrested.

JAMIE. It'll be worth it! Three! *(Rushes at SPENCER who Exits quickly.)*

(ALBERTINE and MILLICENT pop up again outside the window and applaud as KAY comes in from kitchen and JAMIE closes the door.)

MILLICENT. Bravo! Bravo!

ALBERTINE. What a great scene. You could play in ROCKY XII. *(They disappear.)*

KAY. I couldn't get them to leave their loge seats.

JAMIE. *(Goes to window U.R.)* I'm going to hire a plane to write "Spencer Is A Fraud" up and down the coast.

KAY. You can't afford a plane.

JAMIE. *(Sinks on windowseat.)* And if I did it would rain and no one could read it.

KAY. *(Goes to him.)* Would it hurt to go along with him to see what happens?

JAMIE. If you get invited to dinner with a crocodile you might find out you're the dinner.

KAY. *(Sits by him.)* You've been reading "Picturesque Speech" in the *Reader's Digest* again.

JAMIE. What were those two doing outside the window?

KAY. They heard Leyton's voice but they wanted to see what he looked like.

JAMIE. Were they expecting Sydney Greenstreet?

(ALBERTINE and MILLICENT Enter.)

ALBERTINE. *(as she Enters)* He would have been better. This Spencer Leyton looks totally wrong.

JAMIE. What do you mean?

ALBERTINE. No black hat. The villian should always wear a black hat.

MILLICENT. *(Crosses to the desk.)* And those clothes weren't ominous enough. He needs a good costume designer.

ALBERTINE. A ring. He should be wearing a large pinky ring.

MILLICENT. With a diamond in it. And shoes with

pointed toes. *(Sits in desk chair.)*

ALBERTINE. Perhaps I should send him an anonymous letter.

JAMIE. There's been too much writing already.

KAY. But he definitely is a villian.

ALBERTINE. Oh, don't mistake what I'm saying. He's perfect casting.

MILLICENT. And he's playing his part very well. Any reviewer would give him an "arresting" or a "depth of character."

KAY. But in real life what he gets is the property down there.

JAMIE. *(Rises and goes D.R.)* He'll admit to the press he's Willis Waxman and bask in glory. I'll see him on the cover of *People* magazine when I'm a bag boy at the Piggly-Wiggly Supermarket.

MILLICENT. So Spencer Leyton gets everything he wants and Jamie gets nothing. Where's the justice in all this? It's just not fair.

ALBERTINE. *(Crosses to MILLICENT.)* It's like an act curtain in a play. Everything looks impossibly bad but there's always another act.

KAY. This isn't a play.

ALBERTINE. But it could be. We have a hero, a villain, a lovely ingenue, and a foreclosing mortgage. What could be better?

JAMIE. *(Sits D.R.)* I wish I wasn't in the cast.

ALBERTINE. *(with a glint in her eye)* What an opportunity.

MILLICENT. Albertine, what are you thinking?

ALBERTINE. Here is a stranded acting company with no

performance today. The rest of the cast is down on the beach probably playing charades because actors have to act.

MILLICENT. *(Rises as she gets the idea.)* Albertine, how exciting. *(to the others:)* We are excellent at improvisations. You've seen that already.

KAY. *(Rises and goes to JAMIE.)* What are you saying?

ALBERTINE. That we will rewrite the future for you.

MILLICENT. *(Crosses in.)* We will get out talented company out from under their Coppertone and put on a show for Mr. Spencer Leyton that he won't soon forget.

JAMIE. You can't do that. This is life we're living. A little acting can't change it.

ALBERTINE. A *little* acting?

MILLICENT. *(Moves in.)* Did I hear my ears? Young man, we will not do a "little acting." We're talking Academy Awards here.

JAMIE. I'm not so sure you should—

ALBERTINE. We're dying on the vine. Actors must act.

MILLICENT. This is manna from heaven.

KAY. What will you do exactly?

MILLICENT. How do we know now? But whatever it is prepare yourself for shimmering brilliance. They said that about my performance in *"Blithe Spirit."*

ALBERTINE. *(Goes to the door.)* We'll go and tell the company the whole story and then plan our tactics.

JAMIE. *(rises)* When will you let us know what's going to happen?

MILLICENT. *(to ALBERTINE:)* We'd better not tell them anything.

ALBERTINE. Amateurs and professionals never mix. Jamie, dear, you can't possibly expect to keep up with what might transpire so I think the less you know the better.

MILLICENT. Just play it moment to moment and be natural. Go along with whatever happens.

ALBERTINE. You're a very nice boy but you don't have our years of experience.

KAY. *(Goes to MILLICENT.)* I played Emily in *"Our town"* in high school.

MILLICENT. There isn't a girl in these United States who hasn't done that "Goodbye, Grovers Corners" speech, but I'm sure you were charming.

JAMIE. Don't we get a hint what you're going to do?

MILLICENT. You'll have to wait until the curtain rises.

JAMIE. Will it happen here?

MILLICENT. I guess so. What do you think, Albertine?

ALBERTINE. *(Crosses in looking over the room.)* This is a good set for a play. Yes, we'll use this.

KAY. *(Goes towards her.)* Shall I be here?

ALBERTINE. Of course. You're the romantic interest.

JAMIE. Spencer will be absent.

MILLICENT. Oh, he'll be here.

JAMIE. Why?

MILLICENT. Young man, I have played wicked women that make Bette Davis seem like Shirley Temple. *(Goes below JAMIE.)* If I want Spencer Leyton here *(Laughs seductively and turns to JAMIE.)* he will be here.

ALBERTINE. *(Opens door.)* Just leave everything to us.

You two go out and have a nice dinner someplace.

JAMIE. If they haven't put a stopper on my Diner's Club Card.

ALBERTINE. And we'll get to work.

JAMIE. When will we see you again?

ALBERTINE. You be here by eight o'clock and then the next scene will start.

MILLICENT. *(Starts to pull her out.)* Come on, Albertine.

ALBERTINE. Wait!

MILLICENT. What for?

ALBERTINE. We need a curtain line as we exit, don't we?

MILLICENT. How about a "We'll cut them off at the pass!" That's always a good one.

ALBERTINE. No. I have it. "Like a boomerang, we shall return. In the meantime, kiss her your fool!" *(Looks at them and crosses in.)* Well, kiss her, you fool! *(He does.)* There. Curtain! *(They rush out as CURTAIN.)*

Scene 2

That evening just before8:00 P.M. JAMIE is standing by the desk looking through the local phone book. He finds the number and dials. Into phone.

JAMIE. Albertine Johnson, please ... No, I don't know the room number ... Yes, the actress ... How long ago did she leave? ... With whom? ... How big a group? ... They were what? ... full of hilarity, I see ... No, no message, it's too late. *(hangs up)* Much too late. *(Crosses D.C.)* Oh, why didn't I become a sky diver. At least they have parachutes. My rip cord is pulled and nothing's happening.

(KNOCK on door.)

JAMIE. What have I gotten myself into? *(At the door.)* Who is it?

KAY. *(Offstage)* Kay McNaughton, hungry girl fianceé. Has it started yet?

(JAMIE opens the door to KAY.)

JAMIE. Nothing has started. I am all alone.

KAY. I didn't want to miss anything. *(Kisses him lightly and goes down C.)*

JAMIE. I decided to call the whole thing off. I phoned the hotel.

KAY. You didn't?

JAMIE. I just said I did, but Albertine had already gone out and not alone.

KAY. She must have Millicent with her.

JAMIE. And the others.

KAY. How many others?

JAMIE. The operator didn't say. *(Goes to her.)* Kay, I am having a premonition.

KAY. Good or bad?

JAMIE. *(His arms around her.)* Complete and utter disaster. I mean, we don't know what that old girl is up to. We can't have odd people rushing in and out and putting on some kind of an act. They think this is an old-fashioned meller-drammer and they'll throw fake snow in the door. *(Grabs her hand and starts for the door with her.)* Come on, let's go. I'll buy you a Big Mac.

KAY. *(Stops him.)* You are spineless.

JAMIE. Am not. *(Turns and puts her hand on his back.)* Here, feel — spine and requisite number of vertebrae.

KAY. Someone is finally trying to help us so why do you want to abandon ship?

JAMIE. Because my life jacket says "Titanic." Come on. *(Pulls her again.)*

KAY. *(Stops again.)* Jamie Durwood, stop. Are you going to let Spencer foreclose without putting up a fight?

JAMIE. Yes.

KAY. No, you're not. We're past any normal help and out of the blue along comes Albertine and her troupe. Maybe it's all disastrous as you say but then again maybe not. Give them a chance.

JAMIE. Have you envisioned the possibilites? They might make complete fools of themselves and of us and it will spread all over town that I hired a bunch of actors and that makes me an A-number-one idiot.

KAY. You're right, let's go. *(Goes below him and pulls him towards door.)*

JAMIE. I don't believe it.

KAY. What?

JAMIE. How easily your mind can be changed. You sounded so great just then telling me off. You were a cross between Juliet and Mrs. Miniver. Then I say two sentences and you agree with me. *(Stops and stands straight.)* We are not leaving.

KAY. You're sure?

JAMIE. Positive.

ALBERTINE. *(From outside window.)* Good. It worked.

JAMIE. *(Goes to desk.)* What are you doing there?

ALBERTINE. *(Her head pops up in window.)* Making sure the coast is clear before we come in. *(To KAY.)* You would make a great actress, dear. That was brilliant.

KAY. You noticed.

ALBERTINE. I couldn't help it.

JAMIE. Noticed what?

ALBERTINE. How she managed to get you to stay when you wanted to leave.

JAMIE. She didn't get me to stay. I changed my mind.

ALBERTINE. You were going, she agreed, and so you stayed. She knew how to make you remain, didn't you, Kay?

JAMIE. *(to KAY:)* Did you?

KAY. *(Sits on sofa.)* In college, my major was English but my minor was psychology.

JAMIE. You women sure stick together. I must say — *(Turns to window but ALBERTINE is gone.)* She's gone.

KAY. She didn't have a good exit so I think we're going to get a good entrance.

JAMIE. *(Goes towards door.)* I don't trust all this theatre business.

KAY. Go and open the door and play along with her.

JAMIE. *(Goes to door.)* It better be a brilliant entrance

line. *(Opens door and no one is there.)* She's not here.

ALBERTINE. *(From kitchen archway, assuming a very tough act.)* Hands up! Don't move a muscle or I'll waste you!

KAY. Albertine!

JAMIE. *(turns)* What the — ?

ALBERTINE. *(relaxing)* Surprise is the best entrance of all. Did you like that line, "Don't move a muscle or I'll waste you?"

KAY. Authentic.

JAMIE. *(Sits in chair down R.)* Terse.

ALBERTINE. The hit man said that in one of those TV series I did a guest spot on. I was his mother and he tossed me off the Brooklyn Bridge at the opening.

KAY. How terrible.

ALBERTINE. Worse than you think. He did it before the credits.

JAMIE. That's bad?

ALBERTINE. Dear boy, that means it was before the opening commercial and while everyone was either getting a beer or going to the bathroom.

(The front door bursts open and MILLICENT is there with a similar tough act.)

MILLICENT. Hands up! Don't move a muscle or I'll waste you!

JAMIE. What?

KAY. Another one.

ALBERTINE. *(condescendingly)* No, no, no. Millicent, dear. They already heard that line. I just said it. *(Sits in desk chair.)*

MILLICENT. Really?

ALBERTINE. And just a touch more convincingly than you.

MILLICENT. I doubt that.

ALBERTINE. Anyway, it's my line. It's from that episode of *"Gun Vs. Gun."*

MILLICENT. *(Goes down C.)* But that same speech was in *"Shot for Shot."* when I did it.

ALBERTINE. Did you say it?

MILLICENT. No, I was the society matron he was having an affair with so he pushed me off the Golden Gate Bridge.

ALBERTINE. Mine was the Brooklyn Bridge. *(They laugh.)*

MILLICENT. They can't come up with a new idea every week. But, seriously, which of us did say the line better?

ALBERTINE. Yes, with more depth and feeling.

KAY. Well—

JAMIE. *(Rises and moves below chair.)* It was the same line but each of you had a different characterization and I could see a different background to each character as you plumbed the depths of your souls.

MILLICENT. *(laughing)* All right.

ALBERTINE. Very tactful, I must say.

MILLICENT. You don't write reviews for the New Yorker, do you?

JAMIE. *(Sits by KAY and takes her hand.)* Hardly.

MILLICENT. Now that my talent is warmed up, I'll get that Spencer Leyton down here.

JAMIE. For what? We don't understand what you're going to do.

ALBERTINE. *(as MILLICENT goes through book above desk)* You'd never be able to act along with us so you just do what comes naturally.

JAMIE. Like I'm on Candid Camera?

ALBERTINE. You got it.

KAY. *(to MILLICENT:)* Spencer's number is 2435.

MILLICENT. *(dials)* Thanks.

JAMIE. *(Worried, goes C.)* What's she going to say to him?

ALBERTINE. *(Goes to him.)* She does phone conversations beautifully. I do, too, of course. In *"Come Back, Little Sheba"* when I called my mother — oh, heart-breaking. I think I can still remember some of it.

MILLICENT. Not now. I'm getting into character.

ALBERTINE. Sorry.

MILLICENT. *(into phone in a very efficient voice)* Spencer Leyton, please, this is Jacqueline Babbitt calling ... oh, I'm glad you are home, Mr. Leyton. I am calling for Jamie Durwood of Durwood Enterprises ... No, I'm the new secretary. The other unfortunate girl was fired.

KAY. I still work here.

MILLICENT. *(into phone)* Mr. Durwood wishes you to come to his place where he will sign any papers you wish signed to consummate your deal for the shopping mall.

JAMIE. I won't sign.

ALBERTINE. Shh!

MILLICENT. *(into phone)* Yes, tonight. He says no bad publicity and he will go along with you for a percentage

... you can't speak to him right now, he's ... he's ... *(Looks around for help.)*

JAMIE. Drunk.

MILLICENT. *(into phone)* He's not feeling well ... *(Puts on a low, sexy voice.)* To be honest, Mr. Leyton, we've been celebrating his hiring me and he doesn't seem to hold his martinis too well ... Yes, he's known me for quite some time ... *(with a glance to the others)* Yes, it is unusual for a secretary to work at night, but I'm used to night work.

ALBERTINE. She was Lauren Bacall's understudy for awhile.

MILLICENT. *(Sits in chair while still on phone.)* I do anything I can to help my employer ... Yes, Mr. Leyton I do type ... Perhaps we can discuss it later, but do hurry now before Mr. Durwood changes his mind ... I've got the black coffee on ... Bye for now. *(Hangs up as others applaud.)*

ALBERTINE. Can't resist throwing in the sexy other woman, can you?

MILLICENT. Audiences love it. He loved it.

JAMIE. And Spencer is coming here?

MILLICENT. By now he is turning on his ignition.

KAY. I think you turned on his ignition.

MILLICENT. What a nice thing to say, dear.

JAMIE. But I have no intention of selling out.

ALBERTINE. We know, but we had to get him here somehow. It's Plan A.

KAY. What happens when he does get here?

ALBERTINE. Then we go into full speed ahead.

JAMIE. *(Crosses to KAY.)* I'm nervous.

KAY. So am I.

ALBERTINE. We all get stage fright before a performance.

JAMIE. Even you?

ALBERTINE. All of us.

(From outside window, the head of JOYCE INGALLS appears. She is a typical ingenue and very pretty and eager. At the moment, she, too, is very nervous.)

JOYCE. Especially me.

JAMIE. Who is that?

ALBERTINE. This is our ingenue, Joyce Ingalls.

JOYCE. That's my stage name. My real name is Elizabeth Taylor so I had to change it.

MILLICENT. You shouldn't be seen yet, Joyce. You're part of Plan B.

ALBERTINE. *(to JAMIE and KAY:)* That's in case Plan A fails.

JOYCE. I have some quick questions to ask.

ALBERTINE. All right, dear. Go to the back door and Millicent will meet you.

JOYCE. Thank you. *(to others:)* This is my first summer tour and I didn't realize the fringe benefits. *(Head disappears and MILLICENT goes into kitchen.)*

ALBERTINE. That window has better programs than CBS.

JAMIE. *(Sits on sofa.)* What's she supposed to do?

ALBERTINE. *(Moves above sofa.)* We don't give away our plots. Joyce is a very nice girl and a good little actress. You should see her scene where she tells the old man off when he tries to seduce her. She got a hand in Albuquerque.

KAY. She must have been pleased.

ALBERTINE. Of course, I got a good review there, too. *(Goes R. of chair R.)* The morning paper said I was, let me see if I can remember, "stunning and dynamic."

(MILLICENT Enters with JOYCE.)

MILLICENT. That was my review, Albertine, dear. Yours was "interesting and entertaining."

ALBERTINE. I must have gotten them confused.

MILLICENT. You must have. *(Turns back to JOYCE.)* I'd like to present Joyce Ingalls, the ingenue in our company. Joyce, this is Kay McNaughton.

KAY. *(Goes below JAMIE to her.)* It's nice of you to help us out.

MILLICENT. And Jamie Durwood.

JAMIE. *(rises)* Do you know what you're supposed to do this evening?

JOYCE. I know the basic plot and the rest is ad-lib. I wish I were George Burns.

MILLICENT. But the male half of the company is glad you're not.

JOYCE. Millie, you're wicked.

MILLICENT. Only if the part demands, it, dear.

JOYCE. I'm a little nervous performing without a script.

ALBERTINE. Now, what's your problem, Joyce? We don't have time to rehearse. That Spencer Leyton will be here in a few minutes if Millicent was good enough on the phone.

JOYCE. I'm sure she was. *(to MILLICENT:)* I'm sure you

were. *(to others:)* She just has to see a phone and she's off into a character right away. She's better than Lily Tomlin. Why, in our play, *"Sex Marks The Spot."* she has a telephone scene that has the audience screaming. You see, her husband thinks that she—

ALBERTINE. Joyce, we can compliment Millie some other time.

MILLICENT. *(Crosses by desk chair.)* I'm enjoying it right now.

ALBERTINE. Joyce, you're clear on what you're to do?

JOYCE. *(Goes to her.)* Yes, but my character's background—

ALBERTINE. *(to KAY and JAMIE:)* Why don't you two go into the kitchen and make some fudge or something?

MILLICENT. You shouldn't hear the plot.

JAMIE. *(Goes to kitchen.)* Maybe I should get a whiskey. According to Millicent I'm a lush.

KAY. *(Goes to kitchen.)* I'll make coffee.

JOYCE. Mr. Durwood.

JAMIE. *(Stops in archway.)* Yes.

JOYCE. I'll do everything I can to help you. I thought *"Inez"* was a sensational book. What a woman she was. And the things she did. When Inez was with that Spanish nobleman and he attacked her under that El Greco painting—

ALBERTINE. Joyce, later.

JOYCE. Yes. Sorry. *(to JAMIE:)* We'll see you get your mother's royalties.

JAMIE. I don't know how, but thanks. *(JAMIE and KAY Exit.*

ALBERTINE. *(Sits in chair.)* Now, what's your problem?

JOYCE. This is so different from drama school. I feel I'm under-rehearsed if we haven't rehearsed at all.

MILLICENT. *(Goes to her.)* It's the same as the improvs we do at parties.

ALBERTINE. It's the same as charades.

JOYCE. I've been thinking of what to bring on with me.

MILLICENT. Nothing. We don't need props.

JOYCE. I mean what characteristics. Perhaps I was run over by a skate board when I was a child and I limp a bit. *(demonstrates)* Or my hand was caught in a machine when I was in prison, caught in a jute mill or—

ALBERTINE. Joyce, dear, none of this matters, just play the moment.

JOYCE. How about tears? *(starts crying)* I'm very good with tears. When I was on that soap opera, *"Edge of the World,"* I cried every day for five weeks *(now sobbing)* until I was caught in that cement mixer and ended up in the foundation of the library. *(tears verge on hysterics)*

ALBERTINE. Just tears, Joyce. Tears are very good, but not unbridled hysteria.

MILLICENT. You're damn good on stage so think of this as a stage.

JOYCE. *(looks around)* Yes, this is just like a stage setting. I can act here *(Rises and quotes dramatically.)* "Goodbye, world, goodbye, Grover's Corners."

ALBERTINE. *(her arm around JOYCE)* Joyce, dear, we know everyone from you to Kay in there has played Emily in *"Our Town."* Just think of this character you're playing now.

JOYCE. But suppose you don't get to Plan B?

ALBERTINE. *(Sits on sofa with JOYCE.)* If Plan A works, all will be well.

JOYCE. Then I won't have a chance to act at all.

MILLICENT. *(Perches on the C. arm of the sofa.)* Consider you closed out of town.

JOYCE. This will be exciting, won't it? Acting in the real world. But, oh, dear—

ALBERTINE. Yes?

JOYCE. Suppose we do get to Plan B and it's time for me to come on and — oh, my goodness—

MILLICENT. And what?

JOYCE. And I don't feel like it? What happens if I don't feel the part?

ALBERTINE. You come on anyway or I shall cough during all your laughs for the rest of the tour.

JOYCE. You wouldn't?

MILLICENT. And I shall come downstairs in time to cut your act two exit applause.

JOYCE. You wouldn't?

MILLICENT and ALBERTINE. *(sing-song)* Oh, yes, we would!

JOYCE. Theatre is a cruel business, isn't it?

MILLICENT and ALBERTINE. Ars gratia artis!

(Loud KNOCKING on door.)

SPENCER. *(off stage)* Hello, hello in there.

ALBERTINE. *(Rises and takes JOYCE U.C.)* It's him.

JOYCE. Oh, my goodness.

MILLICENT. *(Calls into kitchen in loud whisper.)* Spencer

Leyton is here.

JOYCE. Where is off stage for me?

MILLICENT. Out the back and don't come in until you're cued for Plan B.

SPENCER. *(off stage)* Open up. I don't have all night.

(As JAMIE and KAY rush in and go to windows U.R. to look out.)

JOYCE. I'll get into character in the garden.

JAMIE. What do we do now?

ALBERTINE. *(as she and MILLICENT are at kitchen archway)* Play it as it happens.

MILLICENT. Let him in and be natural.

JAMIE. I'm no actor.

KAY. All I ever did was *"Our Town."*

JOYCE. Me, too. "Good bye, world, — "

KAY and JOYCE. "Good bye Grover's Corners"—

MILLICENT. No time for that. *(To JOYCE.)* You're off! *(Pushes JOYCE into the kitchen.)*

JAMIE. I hope we do well.

ALBERTINE. Remember we're the stars. *(She and MILLICENT Exit kitchen.)*

SPENCER. *(off stage)* Let me in!

KAY. I guess you'd better open the door.

JAMIE. Here goes. *(opens door)*

SPENCER. It's about time.

JAMIE. *(In his best "acting" tone.)* Why, Spencer Leyton, what a surprise. Long time no see.

(SPENCER comes in and JAMIE closes door.)

SPENCER. I understand that you have changed your mind. Very wise of you, my boy. *(Sees KAY.)* What are you doing here? I thought you were fired.

KAY. I've been rehired.

SPENCER. Then where is Jacqueline Babbitt?

JAMIE. Who?

SPENCER. Jacqueline Babbitt. She telephone me.

(ALBERTINE and MILLICENT peek in the open window.)

JAMIE. I don't know any Jacqueline Babbitt. Do you, Kay?

KAY. A Jacqueline Bassett but no Babbitt.

SPENCER. What is going on here? Someone phoned me, someone with a very sensuous voice.

MILLICENT. Ah!

ALBERTINE. Shh! *(SPENCER turns and they duck. KAY clears throat as a cover up.)*

SPENCER. And she said that you had changed your mind and were willing to cooperate with me.

JAMIE. This isn't April Fool's Day, is it?

SPENCER. I don't like being made a fool of. This is your last chance, Durwood. Join me in the shopping mall or I foreclose on Monday. It's too bad about those *"Inez"* royalties. They're going to be big and we could have shared them.

JAMIE. That does it. Now get out of here.

SPENCER. *(Goes below him to door.)* You've had it. Nothing and no one can save you now. *(Opens door.)*

(ALBERTINE speaks from kitchen archway.)

ALBERTINE. Oh, yes, someone can save him.

SPENCER. Who the devil are you?

ALBERTINE. The person who holds the answer to everything.

KAY. Then you must be—

JAMIE. Who?

SPENCER. Yes, who the hell are you?

ALBERTINE. You know everything about me and yet you don't recognize me. I am Inez!

CURTAIN

ACT II

A continuation of Act I, Scene 2.

SPENCER. You are Inez?

ALBERTINE. I have never had a problem projecting. Let me repeat. I am Inez.

JAMIE. *(to KAY, trying not to laugh:)* She is Inez!

KAY. *(in shock)* I heard. I heard.

SPENCER. *(Closes door.)* You can't be Inez.

ALBERTINE. Why not?

SPENCER. *(at a complete loss)* Because — because — there is no Inez.

ALBERTINE. *(Crosses down C.)* But there is and here I am.

SPENCER. Inez is fictional. She doesn't exist.

ALBERTINE. Whatever gave you that idea?

JAMIE. Yes, whatever?

ALBERTINE. There are many who know I exist. Of course the majority are men.

SPENCER. I — I don't believe it.

ALBERTINE. *(to JAMIE and hands on his shoulders:)* Jamie. Jamie. Yes, you are Jamie Durwood. You must be.

KAY. He is.

SPENCER. This can't be—

ALBERTINE. Your mother hasn't sent me a snapshot of you since high school graduation.

JAMIE. I didn't—

ALBERTINE. I know. Doris never told you about me, did she?

JAMIE. No, I—

ALBERTINE. *(her fingers on his lips)* I understand. Many mothers have never told their sons about me. *(moves away down C.)* And many sons have never told their mothers about me.

SPENCER. I don't believe any of this.

ALBERTINE. *(Turns; to SPENCER:)* Quiet, please! Let us have a moment of memory.

KAY. Yes, this is very touching.

ALBERTINE. *(to JAMIE:)* Perhaps you remember your mother speaking of her childhood friend, Albertine?

JAMIE. I believe I do, yes.

ALBERTINE. Doris and I did everything together from playing hopscotch to baking peanut penuche.

SPENCER. You said you were Inez not Albertine.

ALBERTINE. *(Her memory mood is broken.)* I'm getting to that. After fourth grade, my mother took us to Spain where she remarried a dreadful sadist and my name was changed to Inez.

KAY. But you kept in touch with Jamie's mother?

ALBERTINE. *(almost forgetting that)* In touch? Yes, yes, of course. Jamie, she must have mentioned hearing from her blood sister, mustn't she? Say she did.

JAMIE. She did.

ALBERTINE. I remember the day we became blood sisters. We pricked our fingers with a hat pin from our Easter bonnets and pressed the fingers together.

SPENCER. Wasn't that Tom Sawyer?

ALBERTINE. Tom Sawyer never wore an Easter bonnet.

(exhausted) Oh, let me sit, I am so weary. *(sits on sofa)* Perhaps a little whiskey? I've tried to give it up but it's hopeless.

JAMIE. I understand.

KAY. I'll get it. *(Exits kitchen.)* It will be just what you want.

ALBERTINE. A sweet child. I was sweet once, eons ago. *(Looks at SPENCER.)* Who are you?

SPENCER. I am Spencer Leyton.

ALBERTINE. You were speaking most unpleasantly as I came in the room.

JAMIE. Unpleasant and loud.

ALBERTINE. I heard you and that's why I went to the back door. You said Jamie was not getting Doris's royalties. Why is that?

SPENCER. Doris didn't write the book. I did.

JAMIE. Mother did write it.

ALBERTINE. Willis Waxman wrote it.

JAMIE. That's him.

SPENCER. That's me.

ALBERTINE. I assume Willis Waxman was a pen name Doris used because the book is so different from her others.

SPENCER. I am Willis Waxman.

ALBERTINE. How did you know all that about me? There are things in that book that no one but Doris Durwood knew.

SPENCER. *(moves C.)* She — she confided in me.

ALBERTINE. She wouldn't have, not Doris, not my blood sister.

SPENCER. But she did.

JAMIE. There are two sides to every story. *(Sits by ALBERTINE.)* Mother wrote *"Inez"* at Spencer's place. Then she died suddenly and he stole her book.

SPENCER. This is ridiculous. *(Crosses to ALBERTINE.)* I don't know who you are or what you're doing here but I do know Inez is a fictional character. *(Goes to door.)* Now I'm getting out of here.

ALBERTINE. *(rises)* Libel!

SPENCER. *(Stops at door.)* What?

ALBERTINE. I am bringing suit for libel.

SPENCER. You wouldn't dare.

ALBERTINE. *(Crosses to him.)* I have contacted the Civil Liberties Union and this is an invasion of privacy as well as downright dirty and I can prove I am Inez. Can you prove anything in that book?

SPENCER. Anyone can write an unauthorized biography.

ALBERTINE. I wouldn't mind Doris making up some of those incidents but I won't stand for that slander from your word processor.

SPENCER. What incidents?

ALBERTINE. What about that Brazilian bordello?

JAMIE. The reviews called that steamier than a sauna.

ALBERTINE. Willis Waxman has no right to say that about me and if you're he, you're going to pay.

SPENCER. *(getting worried)* This is some kind of joke, isn't it?

ALBERTINE. Do you see me laughing?

SPENCER. *(Goes below her to the chair.)* Doris never mentioned Inez was real. *(sits)* She said she was a combination of all the worst women in current fiction.

ALBERTINE. *(Leans against door dramatically.)* And so I am.

JAMIE. What can I say, Spencer? I'm as shocked as you, believe me.

ALBERTINE. *(Crosses above sofa.)* Think how shocked I was. I'm sitting in a sleazy bar in New Orleans just off Basin Street. *(Moves U.C.)* It's stifling hot, the steam in rising from the Mississippi River, the lonesome wail of a trumpet can be heard in the distance playing "Birth of the Blues." I'm sharing a bottle of rot gut with my friend, Blanche DuBois.

SPENCER. Blanche DuBouis is a character in *"A Streetcar Named Desire."*

ALBERTINE. Where the hell do you think Tennessee got the name? She used to baby-sit him in St. Louis.

JAMIE. Yes, I read that in his autobiography.

ALBERTINE. *(surprised)* You did? *(Back to the dramatics.)* Poor Blanche couldn't hold her liquor. She passed out right on top of a book she was reading.*(using the desk as the table and moving C. during speech)* It wasn't any Gideon Bible either. It was *"Inez."* I started looking through it and I saw it was me. But who was Willis Waxman? Then I remembered Doris had mentioned him in her letter. She said she was working with him. I read on. I was shocked. My reputation was in tatters. Did Doris write it under the name of Willis Waxman or did this other person? Was the royalty going to Doris' son? There and then I left New Orleans and hopped a freight to California. I stood there watching Old Man River fade away downstream and I said, "Goodbye, Grovers — New Orleans ..." *(dramatically forgetting herself)* Curtain! *(sinks in desk)*

SPENCER. What curtain?

JAMIE. Albertine — Inez —?

ALBERTINE. *(thinking fast)* Yes, curtains for Inez. It is curtains. I am suffering from an incurable disease. *(coughs)* The end is near. *(Marches to SPENCER.)* And you. You are ruining my last days. *(Calls toward kitchen.)* Where the hell is that whiskey?

(KAY comes rushing in with bottle and glass which she puts on the desk.)

KAY. Coming.

ALBERTINE. And just in time. Dulls the mind, y'know.

JAMIE. *(Goes to KAY.)* Is this wise?

KAY. I hope the brand is all right.

ALBERTINE. Who cares about brands. It's the proof that matters.

SPENCER. *(Rises and goes to ALBERTINE.)* In *"Inez,"* the book, she could drink any man under the table. So, let's see how Inez in real life can do. *(He pours stiff drink from bottle on desk.)*

ALBERTINE. *(to KAY:)* Help.

SPENCER. What?

ALBERTINE. *(recovering)* Help yourself to a snort.

JAMIE. *(rises)* Kay, why did you get that?

SPENCER. *(Hands glass to ALBERTINE.)* Now drink this and it will prove you are Inez.

KAY. Go ahead. It's in the bag. *(Holds up tea bag she has palmed and swings it in front of her so ALBERTINE sees it and SPENCER doesn't.)*

JAMIE. *(moves in)* Oh, it will suit you to a "T." *(Smiles as KAY indicates it is tea in whiskey bottle.)*

ALBERTINE. *(to SPENCER:)* Here's mud in your computer. *(drinks it all down)* Wow!

KAY. *(Goes to windowseat, drops tea bag in plant on the way.)* I couldn't even do that with a Diet Pepsi.

ALBERTINE. *(Pours another shot.)* That didn't even wet the whistle. Cheers. *(drinks)*

JAMIE. Are you satisfied, Spencer? *(Goes to KAY.)*

SPENCER. *(Goes to ALBERTINE'S R.)* I'm not saying I believe you're Inez but I guess you could make a little trouble.

ALBERTINE. A little? *(Rises and goes C.)* I'll take this right to the Supreme Court and don't think I don't know some of them Justices very well, if you know what I mean.

SPENCER. What exactly do you want from me?

ALBERTINE. I want what's right for Jamie. I remember when Doris wrote me after he was born. Oh, the way she carried on. She wanted everything for him. And then, as he grew, her hopes for him grew, college, architecture school, and then the development here — oh, how she wanted him to have that — *(Works up till almost in tears.)* I'd better have another little shot. *(Pours another and rushes above desk for it.)*

JAMIE. She wants you to give Mother her due. You can say Willis Waxman is Doris Durwood, can't he, Inez?

ALBERTINE. *(brightly as if she hadn't thought of it)* Why, yes, what a good idea. Then the money will be Jamie's.

KAY. *(Sits on the windowseat.)* And the development can go ahead.

SPENCER. Me give up the Shopping Mall? No way.

ALBERTINE. You wouldn't make my last days happy?

SPENCER. I'll send you a comic book.

ALBERTINE. I have lost. I wish I had another plan. *(looks to JAMIE)*

JAMIE. Like a Plan B?

ALBERTINE. Exactly. *(Loud as she cues JOYCE in kitchen.)* A Plan B.

JAMIE. *(towards kitchen)* When I design a building I always have a Plan B. *(Says it loudly out kitchen door.)*

(KAY speaks as JOYCE'S head pops up in window L.)

KAY. That's true. He always has a Plan B.

JOYCE. Oh!

(Ducks down as SPENCER turns and her FOOTSTEPS are heard running to front door.)

SPENCER. *(to JAMIE:)* You think about it. To save the bad publicity I'll cut you in for a percentage of the Shopping Mall but that's all. Give me a ring. *(Heads for door.)*

JAMIE. Can't. I haven't paid AT&T.

SPENCER. What is that?

ALBERTINE. What?

SPENCER. There's someone running out there.

KAY. *(rises)* A jogger.

ALBERTINE. It sounds like the animal stampede in *"King Solomon's Mines."*

SPENCER. I never saw it.

ALBERTINE. *(moves C.)* You can rent it. But get the one with Stewart Granger not the one with Richard Chamberlain because that one—

SPENCER. *(annoyed)* Madame.

ALBERTINE. Call me Inez.

SPENCER. I am not interested in film, theatre, or actors.

ALBERTINE. I knew you didn't have one redeeming quality.

SPENCER. What I am interested in is getting out of here.

(SPENCER opens door and JOYCE is there panting for breath.)

SPENCER. Who the hell are you?

JOYCE. You don't recognize me?

SPENCER. I have never seen you before.

JOYCE. Are you sure?

SPENCER. Positive. *(to others)* Who is this?

JAMIE. She's. well, I think—

KAY. Albertine — Inez — you must know. Tell us.

ALBERTINE. *(Turns away and covers her face with her hands.)* No, no, please—

JOYCE. *(trying to see ALBERTINE as she leans from side to side of SPENCER)* Get out of my way. *(goes to ALBERTINE)*

ALBERTINE. No, no, go away.

JOYCE. *(Takes ALBERTINE'S hands away from her face.)* Let me look at you. It is!

SPENCER. Is what?

JOYCE. Mother! *(Throws her arms around her.)*

SPENCER. *(Closes door.)* Where did she come from?

ALBERTINE. *(Wipes tear from her eye.)* Heaven sent her.

JAMIE. *(Crosses to desk.)* Of course, Inez did have a daughter but she gave her up.

ALBERTINE. For Lent.

SPENCER. For what?

ALBERTINE. For Lent. *(Plays her big scene C.)* It wasn't in the book but I was in Rome at the time. It was just after my ordeal at the Hapzburg Palace, remember? I had made my way South and was sitting in the Piazza at St. Peter's. There was a crowd and the Pope came out on that balcony of his. I didn't understand Italian but I knew it was Lent and I would have to give something up. *(to JOYCE:)* I wrapped you in swaddling clothes and left you at the door of a convenient convent. I gave you up for Lent.

JOYCE. Mother!

ALBERTINE. Daughter! *(They embrace.)*

KAY. This is a beautiful scene.

ALBERTINE. Thank you.

SPENCER. I think it's maudlin.

JOYCE. *(Goes to him.)* You're not — can it be — yes, you are my father. Daddy! *(Throws arms around him and he untangles himself.)*

SPENCER. Stop it! Get off me! I am not your father.

ALBERTINE. No, no, child. Not that man. Never.

JAMIE. I would hardly think so.

KAY. That's Spencer Leyton.

JOYCE. I'm so sorry. I thought you must be Daddy.

SPENCER. You mean you haven't told her who her father is?

ALBERTINE. *(fingers to her lips)* I can't say. Royalty!

SPENCER. *(to JOYCE:)* What's your name, Anastasia?

JOYCE. It's Clotilde.

ALBERTINE. *(Makes a face.)* Clotilde?

SPENCER. *(Goes to JOYCE.)* How did you get here?

JAMIE. What is this, a trial?

SPENCER. I think we have enough curiosity to wonder why this child suddenly jogs to your doorstep.

JOYCE. I'm at the college in town. Down there. *(a dramatic gesture down the coast)*

SPENCER. *(Sits in chair.)* I know where the college is.

JOYCE. My tuition was paid anonymously.

ALBERTINE. *(Sits on sofa.)* My wages of sin.

JOYCE. *(Goes D.C. as JAMIE sits at desk.)* I was in the lab doin' biology. I was dissecting a frog. It made me feel queasy. I looked up and there pressed against the windowpane was a face. *(Points to ALBERTINE.)* That face.

ALBERTINE. *(Agrees, with a look to SPENCER.)* This face.

JOYCE. Yes, that face.

ALBERTINE. I couldn't bear to be so close to my daughter and not see her for a moment.

JOYCE. I only saw the face for a flash and then it was gone. After class, I went to the coffee shop and I was sipping a double chocolate frappe with whipped cream and I looked up and there over my straws I saw the face again.

KAY. *(Perches on back of sofa.)* That face.

ALBERTINE. This face.

KAY. Somehow I suddenly knew. Something inside me started calling. "Mother."

ALBERTINE. *(restraining a tear)* Oh, my child. My Chole!

JAMIE. Clotilde.

ALBERTINE. Oh, my Clotilde.

JOYCE. I followed her. I was taken aback when she ventured into the police station.

ALBERTINE. And not for the first time let me tell you.

JOYCE. When she came out I went in and found out what she was doing there.

SPENCER. How did you find out?

JOYCE. I am a woman, Mr. Leyton. When I want to find out something from a man, *(Voice drops to low, sexy Marilyn Monroe.)* I find it out.

SPENCER. I see.

JOYCE. Mother wanted to know where Durwood Enterprises was. I followed. I lost my courage so I jogged for awhile and now here I am. *(meaning two things)* Did I do well?

ALBERTINE. You've done beautifully, better than I expected.

KAY. *(to JOYCE at C:)* You must be exhausted. Would you like something? A drink perhaps?

JOYCE. Oh, no, not alcohol. I read Mother's book. I know how low she sank through alcohol. *(runs to her)* But I forgive you, Mother. I understand.

ALBERTINE. My sweet one.

KAY. *(Crosses to kitchen.)* Perhaps a glass of milk?

JOYCE. *(Goes to her.)* Homogenized and fat-free?

KAY. Exactly. Come with me.

JOYCE. *(to ALBERTINE:)* I don't think I could do

much more right now.

ALBERTINE. You've done quite enough, dear.

JOYCE. It's a far, far better glass of milk I go to now than I have ever known. *(Exits.)*

KAY. What an unusual child. *(Follows her off.)*

SPENCER. She's a mental case.

ALBERTINE. That is my daughter, Chloe-tilde or whatever, you are talking about.

SPENCER. Pschoanalysis. She needs to lie down and have someone listen to her.

ALBERTINE. They'll listen at the trial.

SPENCER. What trial?

ALBERTINE. For libel.

SPENCER. You're back to that again?

ALBERTINE. *(goes C.)* Can't you just see that girl in the witness box, her hair tied back with ribbon, a simple white handkerchief embroidered with her initials pressed to her tear-stained eyes. "Mommy," she will say, "Mommy, what has that dreadful Spencer Leyton done to you? What lies has he written under the name of Willis Waxman?" she'll say. *(Goes to the sofa above SPENCER.)* "And how he has hurt me," the tears will be cascading down her cheeks now. "My rich fiancé's parents called off the wedding when they found out I was the daughter of the notorious Inez." *(Goes to his R. and points to him.)* Then Clotilde will point in your face. "That man has ruined us" and then she will faint.

SPENCER. I don't care if she has a catatonic fit. No one will believe her. *(rises)*

ALBERTINE. When she hits the floor in a dead faint, those twelve angry men will vote "Guilty!"

JAMIE. No doubt of it.

SPENCER. I don't believe it. You went down to the college and hired some student in the drama club. *(moves C.)* What the hell was that line, "It is a far, far, better glass of milk?" Oh, come now. She is not a very good actress.

ALBERTINE. *(Rushes to him in all honesty.)* Don't tell her that. Don't ever say that to her. You'll break her heart.

JAMIE. I think the poor child was under such stress she wasn't sure what she was saying.

ALBERTINE. Yes, stress. *(Goes to JAMIE.)* Do you have any Valium?

JAMIE. No.

SPENCER. *(Without thinking, his hand goes into his pocket and he pulls out a small prescription phial.)* I do.

ALBERTINE. You have Valium? *(Takes phial.)* Why, Mr. Leyton, do you have a prescription?

SPENCER. Yes, I—

ALBERTINE. Do you take drugs often? *(He takes phial back.)* Are you addicted? This is great news. Before the trial, I'd advise you to check into the Betty Ford Clinic.

SPENCER. *(Goes to door.)* It won't wash, Jamie. You can bring in all the people you want, but the foreclosure is Monday. By the time anything comes to trial you will be on the unemployment line and I shall be cutting the ribbon at the Leyton Shopping Mall right down there.

JAMIE. *(Rises and goes below ALBERTINE to D.C.)* I was hoping something would prevent that.

ALBERTINE. It will. Believe me, it will.

SPENCER. I am now leaving. Again. Every time I open this door someone prevents me from leaving. If anyone is there this time I shall kick him out of the way.

(SPENCER opens door and MILLICENT is there.)

MILLICENT. How do you do.

SPENCER. What the hell?

JAMIE. Go on, spencer, kick her in the shins.

SPENCER. *(to MILLICENT:)* Out of my way.

MILLICENT. You get out of my way. *(Pushes him aside and comes into the room. To JAMIE.)* I take it you are Willis Waxman.

JAMIE. Not quite.

MILLICENT. *(Charges on SPENCER.)* Then you must be Willis Waxman.

SPENCER. I am Spencer Leyton. *(Slams out the front door.)*

ALBERTINE. *(to JAMIE:)* He'll be back. This is what's called a double-take.

SPENCER. *(Comes back in.)* No, I am Willis Waxman. I mean, I am both Leyton and Waxman. Who are you?

MILLICENT. I am your publisher, H.L. Barrister.

SPENCER. But you're a woman.

MILLICENT. *(Strikes a provocative pose.)* Am I?

ALBERTINE. Shall we take a vote? All who think that is a woman raise your hand. *(They all do including MILLICENT but not SPENCER.)*

MILLICENT. *(glaring at him)* Well?

SPENCER. Oh, yes. *(Raises his hand.)*

MILLICENT. There. That's settled. I must say, Mr.

Leyton, or Waxman — will you put your hand down? — *(He does.)* I have delt with many authors in my day but you are taking eccentricity to a new height.

SPENCER. You've surprised me coming here.

MILLICENT. According to the sign outside I am in the home and office of a Jamie Durwood. If you can't introduce me, I shall introduce myself. I am H.L. Barrister. *(They shake.)*

JAMIE. Please to meet the best publisher in the U.S.

MILLICENT. Correct. *(to ALBERTINE as she crosses below JAMIE and JAMIE goes above sofa:)* H.L. Barrister here.

ALBERTINE. Albertine Johnson here.

MILLICENT. Isn't there a great actress by that name?

ALBERTINE. Yes, there is. A brilliant actress but, alas, I am not that talented thespian. I am just a coincidence. I changed my name. Now I am becoming famous as—

SPENCER. Stop!

ALBERTINE. What?

SPENCER. Let's not open a can of worms.

MILLICENT. *(to ALBERTINE:)* You were saying?

ALBERTINE. Just that I am—

SPENCER. *(Goes to MILLICENT.)* Miss Barrister.

MILLICENT. Ms.

SPENCER. Ms. Barrister, what are you doing here? How did you know I was here? Is something wrong?

MILLICENT. *(withering him)* Do you want a, b, c or all of the above?

JAMIE. *(to MILLICENT as he goes R. of chair:)* Please do sit down.

MILLICENT. *(Crosses and sits on sofa.)* Thank you. Am I to assume you are son to Doris Durwood?

JAMIE. Yes, I am and—

MILLICENT. A good author, not great but good and dependable. Somewhere she had a best-seller in her.

JAMIE. I know. I—

ALBERTINE. Have a drink? *(Indicates her bottle.)*

MILLICENT. I never drink on duty.

JAMIE. Are you on duty?

MILLICENT. Always. Best-sellers don't just happen, you know. Editors make books and I have turned some of the worst trash into number ones. *(to SPENCER:)* Not yours, however. Very little editing. *"Inez"* was the best trash that ever came across my desk. After the first three pages I knew it was bucks in the bank.

SPENCER. *(Crosses to sofa.)* Thank you. Ms. Barrister, we have met before somewhere, haven't we?

MILLICENT. I'm sure not. I never forget a face or a handwriting.

SPENCER. You seem so familiar.

ALBERTINE. *(Attempts to cover up.)* She looks like the Cosmopolitan Woman.

JAMIE. How did you ever find him here?

MILLICENT. He almost ran me over.

SPENCER. I did?

MILLICENT. I was getting out of my rented T-Bird when you came speeding out of your driveway. I followed you just as I've seen on television. Tailed, I believe is the proper euphemism.

SPENCER. Now that you've found me, let's get out of here and go down to my club for a drink. *(MILLICENT glares.)* That's right, you never drink on duty. *(Sits beside her.)*

MILLICENT. *(to others:)* You will forgive us for a moment if we talk business, won't you?

JAMIE. *(Sits in chair R.)* Of course. We're very interested.

ALBERTINE. *(Perches C. arm of sofa.)* You wouldn't believe how interested.

MILLICENT. Oh, yes, I would.

ALBERTINE. *(agreeing, to JAMIE:)* Yes, she would.

MILLICENT. *(to SPENCER:)* I'm on my way to Los Angeles and this jaunt to see you is a little tax-deductible side trip. Among other deals, I am going to discuss in L.A. is a mini-series of *"Inez."*

SPENCER. For television?

MILLICENT. Not for Marvel Comics.

ALBERTINE. A mini-series will mean a lot of money for the author, won't it?

SPENCER. *(rises)* We must discuss this in the quiet of my pine-paneled study.

MILLICENT. There's a hitch.

SPENCER. *(sits again)* I knew it.

ALBERTINE. Goodie.

MILLICENT. We must reveal who Willis Waxman is. The producers will want to do a big announcement of the series, a press party with the stars kissing the author, author shaking hands with director all the usual friendly things before they start knifing each other in private.

JAMIE. So Willis Waxman will be revealed as Spencer Leyton?

MILLICENT. Correct.

ALBERTINE. *(rises, to SPENCER:)* Then you'll have to raise your ante.

SPENCER. What ante?

MILLICENT. What is she talking about?

ALBERTINE. *(Puts on a tougher characterization.)* Come now, we're all mature adults, aren't we?

JAMIE. I wonder.

ALBERTINE. You and the author here are in this together, aren't you, for the moolah?

MILLICENT. Moolah?

ALBERTINE. *(Glares at her, almost breaking.)* Dough, cash, money.

MILLICENT. Oh, that moolah.

ALBERTINE. *(Goes to desk for bottle.)* That's what I said. Spencer here has been helping me out financially, if you know what I mean.

MILLICENT. You're his mistress?

SPENCER. Good God, no!

ALBERTINE. No way.

SPENCER. I haven't given her a cent.

ALBERTINE. You see how badly he lies. You better not let him take the witness stand.

MILLICENT. What are you talking about?

ALBERTINE. *(Goes C with the bottle.)* Spencer has been giving me money to keep him out of court. If *"Inez"* is going to be a mini-series it will make even more money so Spencer had better raise his payments to me.

MILLICENT. You mean you're blackmailing him?

ALBERTINE. You got it. *(Swigs from bottle.)*

SPENCER. No, it's not true.

JAMIE. They always deny it.

MILLICENT. *(to SPENCER:)* We must go to the police

immediately and expose this wanton woman.

ALBERTINE. Go to the police and your *"Inez"* will be tied up in so much litigation it will never get released to television. *(Bottle goes down on desk.)*

MILLICENT. What is she talking about?

SPENCER. *(Goes to door.)* Let's get the hell out of here.

MILLICENT. *(Goes to ALBERTINE.)* I want to know what you know and don't want me to know that Spencer Leyton knows.

ALBERTINE. He knows who I am.

MILLICENT. Who?

SPENCER. No.

JAMIE. Tell her.

ALBERTINE. I am Inez!

MILLICENT. You!

SPENCER. She isn't!

JAMIE. *(rises)* She is!

ALBERTINE. I am!

MILLICENT. You mean that book is true?

ALBERTINE. Almost all of it.

MILLICENT. What a woman you are. How I envy you.

SPENCER. *(Goes below JAMIE to MILLICENT.)* Wait a minute. She is not Inez. I wrote *"Inez."* It's from my head.

ALBERTINE. He didn't write Inez.

JAMIE. Doris Durwood did.

MILLICENT. Your mother?

JAMIE. Yes.

SPENCER. No.

MILLICENT. Then let me speak to her.

JAMIE. *(Sits on sofa.)* She's dead. You know that.

ALBERTINE. Does anyone know a medium?

MILLICENT. *(Goes to JAMIE.)* What proof have you your mother wrote *"Inez?"*

JAMIE. Well, none really.

SPENCER. You see.

ALBERTINE. I am proof. His mother, Doris Durwood, kept track of me and put it into a book. Take me to a witness stand. I will tell all in a long speech. I will be the witness for the prosecution.

MILLICENT. Let's not be hasty here.

SPENCER. *(Goes to windowseat.)* This is all lies. I wrote it.

MILLICENT. *(Goes to ALBERTINE at desk.)* If you are Inez, prove it.

SPENCER. She can't prove it.

(From off stage, JOYCE'S voice comes as in a struggle.)

JOYCE. No, no, I must tell them the truth.

KAY. *(off stage) Stay here, child.*

MILLICENT. What's that?

ALBERTINE. Proof. That is proof.

JOYCE. *(off stage)* Let me go.

(JOYCE rushes in, followed by KAY.)

JOYCE. Mother.

MILLICENT. Mother?

JOYCE. What are they doing to you?

ALBERTINE. I've faced adversity before.

SPENCER. I wish the San Andreas Fault would open up. *(Foot up on windowseat as he looks out.)*

JAMIE. Under your feet.

MILLICENT. *(to MILLICENT:)* This is your daughter?

ALBERTINE. Yes. Like Stella Dallas, I tried to stay out of Clotilde's life but I, too, failed.

MILLICENT. *(to KAY:)* And who are you?

KAY. I am Kay McNaughton sometimes fianceé. I've been trying to calm this child down.

JOYCE. I will not calm down. I will tell all on the witness stand. That book has lies in it.

ALBERTINE. *(to JAMIE:)* Your mother did embellish hither and thither.

JAMIE. Poetic license.

ALBERTINE. *(Sits desk chair.)* But those embellishments will be worth a fortune to me in court.

SPENCER. *(Goes above sofa.)* She can't prove a thing. I wrote *"Inez"* out of my own head. Every word of it.

MILLICENT. *(Goes to him.)* Unless she can prove you knew her and if you have the original material you wrote then we can laugh Mr. Durwood and that woman out of court. *(Gestures to ALBERTINE.)*

ALBERTINE. No, no! *(JOYCE rushes to her and puts her arms around her.)*

SPENCER. *(Opens front door.)* Come with me and I'll show you the notes and manuscript.

MILLICENT. And leave this bunch of crooks here alone?

SPENCER. Bring them with us.

MILLICENT. *(Goes to him at door.)* I only have a two-seater. You bring the work back here and then we'll call the authorities. Blackmail is a serious offense.

ALBERTINE. *(to JOYCE:)* I hope our goose isn't cooked.

MILLICENT. *(Pushes SPENCER out.)* Hurry!

SPENCER. It won't take five minutes.

JAMIE. The way he drives, three.

SPENCER. *(Comes back and pokes head in door.)* I'm sure I've seen you before somewhere.

MILLICENT. I'm sure not. Go, get the material. Save our necks. *(SPENCER rushes off, she waves after him.)* Godspeed! *(Closes the door. There is a moment of quiet and then they all burst into laughter and MILLICENT sinks into chair R.)*

JAMIE. I don't believe you people.

KAY. *(Goes to JAMIE and sits.)* You're all so talented.

ALBERTINE. Your "Godspeed" line went out with Mary Pickford.

MILLICENT. I couldn't keep a straight face when you said you hoped your goose wasn't cooked.

ALBERTINE. Didn't you like that Stella Dallas bit?

JAMIE. We're going to have to see your play.

MILLICENT. I haven't had such fun since I played *"Born Yesterday." (They brush away the tears.)*

JAMIE. Now, we have to wait for him to come back with the materials.

ALBERTINE. *(Moves C.)* If it's your mother's handwriting we'll keep it. If it's his, we'll destroy it.

MILLICENT. And faced with you as Inez and a libel suit and me as his publisher who will threaten exposing him as a fraud we'll have won.

ALBERTINE. We'd better get some document ready for him to sign before he sees through the sting.

MILLICENT. Hurry.

ALBERTINE. *(Goes to sofa.)* Jamie, you dictate to your just rehired secretary. *(They go to desk, KAY gets typing paper from drawer, and moves chair to typing table. JOYCE goes to sofa.)*

KAY. I'm so nervous.

JOYCE. What will we do till Leyton comes back?

MILLICENT. In a play they would dim the lights to denote the passage of time.

ALBERTINE. And then the lights would come back up as Spencer enters.

KAY. Would it be nice if life were a play?

(LIGHTS dim to black.)

ALBERTINE. *(in blackout)* Ionesco might say that life *is* a play.

JOYCE. Who is Ionesco?

ALBERTINE. Oh, dear.

MILLICENT. Let's just be quiet and wait for Spencer.

(LIGHTS come up as SPENCER knocks on door! JOYCE has sat on sofa, KAY has moved chair back into position by desk and the paper is out of the typewriter and on desk.)

MILLICENT. There we are.

ALBERTINE. Spencer Leyton is back.

KAY. *(to JAMIE as he goes to door:)* Time passes quickly when you're having fun.

MILLICENT. Let's hope he has all the originals with him.

JAMIE. Once we get our hands on them we're in the home stretch. *(Opens door.)*

SPENCER. Sorry I took so long. *(to MILLICENT who rises:)* Here we are. *(Has two large manila envelopes with him.)* The original manuscript and typed notes all dated. There's your proof. *(JAMIE closes the door.)*

MILLICENT. This is what we need.

SPENCER. That should prove everything. That is *"Inez."*

ALBERTINE. *(Goes below sofa to MILLICENT.)* My life is here. *(Grabs the envelope and holds it to her bosom.)* How well-stuffed and full it was... *(to JOYCE:)* I hope you never know everything that is in here.

JOYCE. I read the book, Mother.

ALBERTINE. *(Goes C.)* Lies! Lies! It's not all the truth.

JOYCE. *(Goes to her.)* I'm sure none of it is.

KAY. But some of it must be.

ALBERTINE. Well, here and there. *(Crosses up R. looking in envelopes.)*

JOYCE. *(Follows her.)* I love you and will stand by you, Mother, no matter what.

SPENCER. *(Goes C.)* Can we get down to business? That is my proof. Jamie has none that Doris Durwood wrote a word of that. *(Points at envelopes.)* What's in that envelope is a figment of my imagination. *(Points to ALBERTINE.)* And that Inez coincidence.

ALBERTINE. I deny it.

SPENCER. A lying, cheating, out-for-anything-she-can-get coincidence.

ALBERTINE. Well! *(Sneaks out of room into kitchen area.)*

KAY. *(Goes to SPENCER with paper.)* Be that as it may.

While you were away, a paper was drawn up. As Mr. Durwood's unpaid secretary I think I should show it to you. It says that you will continue the loan for another six months and you will admit that Doris Durwood wrote the book not you, and you will donate all past royalties to the Durwood Enterprises Land Development.

SPENCER. *(laughs)* Who wrote that, Noel Coward?

KAY. Jamie and I wrote it.

SPENCER. *(to MILLICENT:)* They're nuts, aren't they?

MILLICENT. *(Moves below sofa.)* Perhaps not. I mean, all the bad publicity might stop the mini-series and hold up a second printing of the book, but if you sign that your reputation will still be in tact.

KAY. If the trial goes through you'll be shunned like a leper.

JOYCE. *(Crosses above sofa.)* It would make Mother happy knowing the monies went to a good cause.

JAMIE. You'd better sign, Spencer.

SPENCER. *(Takes paper from KAY, crosses to desk and slaps it down.)* My proof is in those notes. You have no notes, nothing to even hint that your mother wrote *"Inez."* Look for yourself in that envelope.

JAMIE. *(Moves in above chair.)* What envelope?

KAY. *(Crosses to SPENCER.)* Yes, what envelope?

JOYCE. I don't see any envelope.

(MILLICENT goes C. as ALBERTINE Enters empty-handed.)

MILLICENT. What have you done with it? We need that proof.

ALBERTINE. The story of Inez is being cleaned up. It's in the washer.

SPENCER. What?

ALBERTINE. In Wisk. It's taking away more than ring around the collar. The pages are crumbling and the words are disintegrating. Your proof is kaput.

MILLICENT. They have won. You'd better sign.

SPENCER. *(Goes C.)* They have not won. The evidence, as you call it, was only Xerox copies of my originals.

ALBERTINE. Xerox?

KAY. *(Sits at desk.)* Oh, no!

JAMIE. *(Crosses above sofa.)* Not the originals?

MILLICENT. Clever boy!

JOYCE. Is that bad, Mother?

ALBERTINE. It's the final curtain. *(JAMIE goes to window-seat as ALBERTINE goes by KAY.)*

SPENCER. So long, Jamie, boy. I am going to sue you for something *(Goes to ALBERTINE.)* and I shall bring blackmail charges against you. *(Goes to JAMIE.)* I shall foreclose one second after midnight on Monday morning. If you want a job as a clerk in one of my stores send me a resume. Ms. Barrister, I suggest we go to a coffee shop where we can have a talk.

MILLICENT. I don't know, I—

SPENCER. *(Goes to door.)* Come along. Perhaps we should go out the back way. There is always someone behind this door, but, no, not this time.

(Opens foor and H.L. BARRISTER stands there. He is middle-aged, efficient, crisp and likable in a business sense.)

SPENCER. I don't believe it.

MILLICENT. Who is it?

SPENCER. What are you doing there?

BARRISTER. I was looking for the bell.

JAMIE. It doesn't work.

BARRISTER. Then I should have knocked.

SPENCER. Just who the hell are you?

BARRISTER. I am H.L. Barrister.

ALBERTINE. What a coincidence.

JAMIE. Barrister?

KAY. *(Rises at same time.)* Not another!

JOYCE. *(Rises at same time.)* What a plot twist!

MILLICENT. *(Slips out.)* Oh, dear!

SPENCER. You can't be H.L. Barrister.

BARRISTER. Why not? I always have been.

ALBERTINE. *(Approaches politely.)* How do you do, Mr. Barrister. It's time we met.

BARRISTER. Who are you?

ALBERTINE. I am actually—

SPENCER. *(Goes below sofa.)* No, she's not.

BARRISTER. Not what?

SPENCER. Not who she says she is.

ALBERTINE. I haven't said who I was.

BARRISTER. That's right, she hasn't.

SPENCER. If you're the real Barrister, then who is she? *(Looks for MILLICENT.)* And where is she?

BARRISTER. She?

SPENCER. The other real Barrister.

BARRISTER. Young man, H.L. Barrister is a man. that's one thing I am sure of. And, I might add, my three ex-wives will corroborate that.

SPENCER. Then who is that other one? *(Points where MILLICENT was.)* She was right there.

BARRISTER. *(Goes below sofa.)* I obviously have broken up some sort of California word game. I'll be on my way if someone will just tell me where Willis Waxman is.

JAMIE. *(Points at SPENCER.)* There.

BARRISTER. You?

SPENCER. *(Goes to him.)* I am Willis Waxman.

BARRISTER. Who is also Spencer Leyton?

JAMIE. You hit it.

BARRISTER. Then I am in deep trouble.

KAY. *(meaning SPENCER)* So is he.

BARRISTER. It appears there is a case of mistaken identity concerning Barristers.

SPENCER. I have been lied to.

JOYCE. *(Crosses into C.)* I am getting very confused. If he is—

KAY. Joyce — Coltilde—

JAMIE. No!

ALBERTINE. *(to JOYCE:)* Why don't you go into the kitchen, dear. *(Pushes her there.)*

JOYCE. Why? It's more fun out here.

KAY. Why don't you devil some eggs?

JOYCE. I don't know how.

KAY. Then we'll make some more coffee. Come along, dear.

JOYCE. *(as they Exit)* There are levels of meaning here I don't quite grasp.

SPENCER. I want to know what's happening.

ALBERTINE. Don't we all?

JAMIE. *(drowning down the growing bedlam)* If everyone

will be calm for a minute.

BARRISTER. *(Sits on sofa trying to be composed.)* I am completely calm. I practice yoga.

SPENCER. How can I be calm when there is an army of H.L. Barristers marching around this living room?

JAMIE. I only see one.

BARRISTER. And I am he.

SPENCER. But there is—

JAMIE. Quiet! Now, Mr. Barrister, if that's who you are.

BARRISTER. It is.

JAMIE. How do you come to be standing outside that door?

BARRISTER. I am on my way to Los Angeles to discuss a mini-series of *"Inez."*

SPENCER. *(Sits by him.)* So is the other one.

BARRISTER. Other who?

SPENCER. Other you.

ALBERTINE. The one he thinks is a woman.

JAMIE. *(Goes above sofa.)* How did you come to my door?

BARRISTER. There was no answer when I stopped at Leyton's address. I was on my way back to the highway when I saw the Durwood Enterprises sign. Then it hit me. Of course. Doris Durwood lived here with her son. He might know where this Spencer Leyton is.

JAMIE. And I do.

SPENCER. *(Rises and goes to door.)* Then let's get out of here and discuss business.

JAMIE. Mr. Barrister.

BARRISTER. Yes.

JAMIE. *(Goes C.)* Since you are Mother's publisher, didn't you notice anything in the style of writing in *"Inez"* that was similar to Mother's?

BARRISTER. I did as a matter of fact, but then Mr. Leyton explained it.

SPENCER. I said how much Doris had helped me in my style, didn't I, Mr. Barrister?

BARRISTER. Exactly. *(to JAMIE:)* Of course, your mother wouldn't have written anything quite so — well, graphic, as *"Inez."*

ALBERTINE. Unless she was writing from fact and not from imagination.

BARRISTER. From fact?

ALBERTINE. Yes, you see—

SPENCER. Time to go.

JAMIE. My mother wrote *"Inez."*

BARRISTER. *(Rises.)* What!

JAMIE. She did.

SPENCER. *(Crosses in.)* She didn't. I did.

BARRISTER. *(Goes to JAMIE.)* This is a very serious charge, young man. Can you prove it?

JAMIE. No, but—

SPENCER. No, he can't.

BARRISTER. This happens all the time. Would-be authors always claim they have written a best-seller but there's no proof.

ALBERTINE. There is this time.

BARRISTER. Where is it?

ALBERTINE. I'm it, I am Inez.

SPENCER. Don't believe her. She's a fraud.

ALBERTINE. I have known Doris Durwood since kindergarten and I have written her my whole life story. I'm ashamed of it but perhaps it will save other girls from taking the wrong steps.

BARRISTER. If this is true—

SPENCER. It isn't.

JAMIE. It is.

BARRISTER. Do you have any proof Doris wrote this?

ALBERTINE. It's in the washing machine.

SPENCER. I have proof at home. I have the originals that I wrote.

JAMIE. Mother wrote them.

SPENCER. It's my typewriter.

BARRISTER. On his typewriter?

JAMIE. That's because she worked up there at his office. You see, this whole thing goes back to my housing development I'm building and a mortgage and a shopping mall and—

BARRISTER. I don't give a damn about shopping malls. I sell books. *(Goes to ALBERTINE.)* You honestly claim you are Inez, that she is a real person?

ALBERTINE. Every single sin of me.

BARRISTER. Then the book is all true?

ALBERTINE. Ah, there's the rub. Some of it is inaccurate. Some of it is wrong and some of it is libel.

BARRISTER. Libel? That is the worst word in the English language. *(Staggers to desk chair where ALBERTINE helps him sit.)*

ALBERTINE. I could forgive Doris Durwood but not this one. *(Points to SPENCER.)* I'll drag him right up to the Supreme Court.

SPENCER. But you can't prove any of it. Let's get out of here.

ALBERTINE. Stop! *(Calls towards kitchen.)* I do have a witness to my shame.

BARRISTER. A witness? Who?

(JOYCE rushes in.)

JOYCE. Me!

BARRISTER. Who are you?

SPENCER. She doesn't matter.

ALBERTINE. *(her arms around JOYCE)* She is my daughter. This is my beloved bastard.

JOYCE. Mummy has broken all ten commandments and made up some of her own to break but she is still my mother. And when she goes to the gas chamber and says, "Goodbye, world, goodbye, Grovers Corners—"

ALBERTINE. That's enough, dear. She gets carried away.

BARRISTER. *(Rises.)* But no one could have led the life Inez did.

JOYCE. Mummy could.

ALBERTINE. And did.

SPENCER. You don't believe them do you?

BARRISTER. *(Crosses below sofa.)* It is right on the edge of farce.

ALBERTINE. *(Goes to him.)* No, no, farce always has closets and mistaken identity and — yes, it does seem to be right on the edge, doesn't it?

BARRISTER. I think this bears some investigation. Come along, Leyton, we'll go to a hotel and make a few phone calls.

KAY. Not yet.

BARRISTER. What?

(KAY is standing in kitchen doorway with tray of coffee.)

KAY. I've just made fresh coffee. *(Puts tray on desk.)*

JAMIE. And just in time.

SPENCER. Not now.

ALBERTINE. Yes. *(Takes BARRISTER by the arm.)* A nice cup of coffee and we'll have a little chat about my wicked life. Wouldn't that be nice?

BARRISTER. I have always wondered about that coupling in Curacao.

ALBERTINE. *(Sits him by herself on sofa.)* That was nothing compared to the night I was lost in the African Veldt with those Watusi warriors. They're so tall.

KAY. *(to SPENCER:)* Mr. Leyton, regular or decaf?

SPENCER. I don't give a damn.

KAY. Sugar or a substitute?

SPENCER. Neither.

KAY. Cream or Coffeemate?

SPENCER. Leave me alone!

JAMIE. Temper, temper. *(Goes to KAY for coffees.)* How about you, Mr. Barrister?

BARRISTER. Just black, please. *(to ALBERTINE:)* This is some kind of a — what do you call it? — put-on, isn't it? You're not really Inez. You're just acting.

ALBERTINE. *(extremely hurt)* No one has ever accused me of "just acting." I have reviews that—

JOYCE. *(To the rescue, crosses C.)* Mummy! *(to BARRISTER:)* She's talking about when she did community theatre work.

ALBERTINE. In prison. Yes, after I was caught shop-lifting that hula hoop. *(JOYCE, in relief, goes to windowseat.)*

SPENCER. You're not swallowing all this?

BARRISTER. She's very convincing. *(JAMIE hands him cup.)* Thank you.

JAMIE. She will make a great witness on the stand. *(Hands cup to SPENCER.)*

SPENCER. No jury will believe you.

(MILLICENT Enters with glass of water and pill bottle.)

MILLICENT. Juries always believe a dying woman.

SPENCER. There! That's her! That's H.L. Barrister.

MILLICENT. I beg your pardon.

BARRISTER. Who is?

SPENCER. She is. There. She said she was you.

MILLICENT. There must be some mistake. I said I am Doctor Belinda Barrister. Here, Inez, take this.

ALBERTINE. Why?

MILLICENT. To keep you going.

ALBERTINE. Oh, yes, of course.

JOYCE. Mummy!

ALBERTINE. *(Takes pill.)* Thank you.

BARRISTER. What's the matter with her?

MILLICENT. Terminal.

JOYCE. *(Collapses on windowseat with a gulp.)* Oh, no!

JAMIE. Inez—

KAY. *(a cup to JAMIE at C.)* Drink this.

SPENCER. This is the end.

ALBERTINE. Not quite yet. *(Hands the glass to MILLICENT.)*

MILLICENT. Another few months if we're lucky. *(Puts the glass on table by sofa.)*

JAMIE. Just till the trial, right?

ALBERTINE. I'll make it till I finish my testimony and then — *(Rises.)* — and then — perhaps I shall collapse right there and how could any jury say anything to Spencer Leyton but—

ALBERTINE and MILLICENT. Guilty! *(ALBERTINE collapses back on sofa gasping.)*

JOYCE. *(in tears)* Dear Mummy has suffered so much.

ALBERTINE. *(Gasps for breath.)* Coffee.

MILLICENT. *(Takes it from KAY at C.)* Here. Inez. Drink this coffee. *(Holds cup out.)* It's one hundred percent Columbian, hand-picked by Maria Consuela in the high mountains of the Andes. *(Getting warmed up to the speech, she turns front.)* This coffee has been tested in the leading restaurants of the United States and Europe and here's what customers say — *(JOYCE has risen during speech and MILLICENT is suddenly aware that they are all staring at her.)* Oh, dear!

SPENCER. That's it! You're it!

BARRISTER. What?

SPENCER. Television. I knew I'd seen you before. She does the pitch for coffee. She's an actress.

BARRISTER. Of course. she hawks things at me from every channel.

MILLICENT. No, no, that's my twin sister.

JOYCE. *(Crosses U.C. being helpful.)* Hypatia.

MILLICENT. *(Stopped dead, turns to JOYCE.)* Hypatia?

JOYCE. I played Hypatia in *"Misalliance"* in Duluth last summer.

SPENCER. They're all actresses. This is a whole rotten troupe.

ALBERTINE. *(Rises.)* Just a minute. Actresses we are but rotten we are not. *(Goes C.)* Oh, I wish I had my reviews with me.

BARRISTER. *(Rises.)* Why are you doing this?

JAMIE. *(Takes cup from MILLICENT and puts on desk.)* They're trying to help me and, I'm afraid, it did get rather overdone.

MILLICENT. But not overacted.

KAY. You must see, Mr. Barrister, they were only trying to convince you of the truth. Jamie's mother did write *"Inez."* Spencer stole it.

SPENCER. This is all a scheme, a sting. they think they're Robert Redford and Paul Newman and they're nothing but a cheap vaudeville turn.

ALBERTINE. That does it! Let me at him! I have my black belt. *(MILLICENT and JAMIE restrain her.)*

SPENCER. Well, Mr. Barrister, now shall we leave?

BARRISTER. I do think you people were rather marvelous. *(Goes below sofa to ALBERTINE.)* You almost convinved me you were Inez.

ALBERTINE. I was good, wasn't I?

BARRISTER. You were remarkable.

(Door bursts open and BUCK RANDALL is there. He is middle-aged, rough and unkept. He is dressed in jeans and a flowered shirt. He is extremely angry.)

BUCK. Albertine, where the hell are you?

ALBERTINE. No!

MILLICENT. *(Backs up towards desk in fright.)* Oh, my God!

JAMIE. You can't bust in here.

KAY. *(same time as above)* Who are you?

SPENCER. *(same time as above)* Another one!

JOYCE. *(same time as above)* It's him!

BARRISTER. *(same time as above)* What now?

BUCK. *(Pushes SPENCER upstage and goes to ALBERTINE and BARRISTER.)* So this is the guy. *(Points at BARRISTER.)*

ALBERTINE. No, Buck, he's an important publisher from New York.

BUCK. Yeah?

BARRISTER. Who is he?

ALBERTINE. This is my ex-husband, Buck Randall.

SPENCER. *(Laughs as he crosses down to BUCK.)* Just another lousy actor.

MILLICENT. She's telling the truth this time.

SPENCER. It's over. We know all about you.

BUCK. *(Knocks SPENCER out of the way.)* Drop it. Buddy.

KAY. *(to JAMIE:)* Is he for real?

JAMIE. I don't know.

JOYCE. *(Goes above sofa.)* I hope he isn't my daddy.

BUCK. I've had a private eye on you, Albertine so I know you've been meeting some dude on the side.

ALBERTINE. We're divorced. Why can't I see someone if I want?

BUCK. Because you'll always be mine.

SPENCER. This is such a rotten script.

BUCK. Shaddup! *(Pulls out revolver, to BARRISTER.)* Get

over there, fella.

ALBERTINE. Buck, you wouldn't—

BUCK. Anyone who trifles with you gets it right in the gut.

BARRISTER. He's just acting. He's not serious, is he?

ALBERTINE. Buck is always serious.

JAMIE. *(Approaches him.)* Now, Mr. Randall, we know you're just an actor and—

BUCK. Drop it!

JAMIE. O.K.

(Wrestles with BUCK and GUN goes off. During the fight, KAY goes above sofa, ALBERTINE throws herself in front of BARRISTER. At the gunshot, they all stop in amazement that it is real. A scream from ALBERTINE and she falls into BARRISTER'S arms. A second later, a scream from JOYCE as she collapses over the back of the sofa.)

BUCK. Let me go, you idiot!

MILLICENT. It went off!

JAMIE. It's real!

BUCK. *(Looks about, sees both women writhing in pain.)* Oh, no, what have I done? *(Rushes out front door.)*

JAMIE. Wait. Come back.

BARRISTER. This woman has been shot.

KAY. *(by JOYCE)* Joyce, she's been shot.

SPENCER. One shot went off and two people are hit. Oh, come, this whole thing is another hoax.

BARRISTER. You're right. One bullet does not make two bodies.

ALBERTINE. *(Recovers and stands up.)* I heard a shot and it was a natural reaction.

JOYCE. *(Stands up.)* I wanted that "Goodbye, Grovers Corners" speech.

MILLICENT. I restrained myself for once.

SPENCER. Didn't the jealous husband bit go out with Howdy-Doody?

BARRISTER. You're right, Mr. Leyton. I'm glad that — *(Sees something in wall right of the U.C. arch.)* What's that?

JAMIE. What?

BARRISTER. *(Crosses to it.)* Here, in the wall. It's a bullet hole. It's fresh. Good Lord, that was a real gun with a real bullet.

ALBERTINE. He is my ex-husband. I know it's asking a lot to believe me after all that's gone on, but there it is, the truth.

BARRISTER. He could have killed me.

SPENCER. Or me.

BARRISTER. You're just an author.

JAMIE. He isn't.

BARRISTER. I don't care whether he wrote *"Inez"* or Doris Durwood wrote it. The fact is that we have a group of actors working free to prove Doris did write it. We have the actress's jealous husband shooting at a prominent publisher, and we have a developer trying to build a shopping mall by foreclosing on some decent people. This is a sensational story. I'll have it in headlines. I'll order another hard-cover printing of *"Inez."* Where is the phone?

JAMIE. *(Points to it.)* There.

BARRISTER. *(Goes to it.)* Never in the history of publishing — *(as dials)*

SPENCER. Wait a minute, Mr. Barrister. This doesn't make me look too good.

BARRISTER. The hell with you. This is business.

SPENCER. But—

BARRISTER. *(Looks in wallet.)* Let me get my phone card.

JAMIE. *(Crosses to him followed by KAY.)* Don't bother. Be my guest.

SPENCER. *(Crosses below sofa.)* This will ruin me. I'll look like another Simon Legree chasing little Jamie across the ice floes.

MILLICENT. *(Goes above sofa.)* You'll rank with Dillinger and Capone and—

JOYCE. The Wicked Witch of the West.

ALBERTINE. Little children will run from you on the streets.

JOYCE. They'll yell after you, "Unclean! Unclean!"

KAY. There is a way out. You can sign this. *(Crosses to him with paper and pen.)*

BARRISTER. *(on phone)* Inquirer? Get me Clifton ... Well, interrupt him. This is page one.

MILLICENT. *(by windowseat)* You'll have to move out of town.

JOYCE. You'll have to disappear.

ALBERTINE. Like Claude Raines in *"The Invisible Man."*

KAY. This paper merely says that you were acting for Doris Durwood and you admit she wrote *"Inez."*

BARRISTER. *(into phone)* Come on, come on—

ALBERTINE. And how all the royalties go to her estate and—

KAY. And you won't foreclose Monday.

SPENCER. I know. You told me all that, but I can't—

BARRISTER. *(into phone)* Ah, there you are. Have I got a story for you. It's sordid, filthy, despicable and great.

SPENCER. I'll sign. I'll sign. *(He does on the table by sofa.)*

BARRISTER. *(into phone)* Hello — hello — it went dead.

KAY. The phone bill!

JAMIE. It's only three months overdue.

BARRISTER. There must be a phone on the corner. *(to SPENCER:)* Let's go to your place.

SPENCER. Not me. Stay away from me. *(Starts backing out.)* I admitted everything. I didn't write *"Inez."* I signed royalties over to Durwood. I made a charity contribution. Maybe it's tax deductible. I don't know. Just leave me alone. All of you. I never want to see you again. I'm moving to Tahiti like Gaugin. *(He is out the door. A moment of stunned silence.)*

ALBERTINE. I think we did it.

MILLICENT. I know we did it.

JOYCE. Were we brilliant?

JAMIE. *(Joins KAY.)* I don't believe it.

KAY. You were incredible. Oh, Mr. Barrister, what must you think?

BARRISTER. You'd be surprised.

(BUCK comes in from the kitchen.)

BUCK. Who says understudies never go on?

JAMIE. What do you mean?

ALBERTINE. *(Goes to BUCK.)* Buck here is general understudy in the company.

BUCK. This is the first time I've gone on during the tour. I was to come in if things got tough and they did.

KAY. And I thought you were real.

JAMIE. *(Moves in.)* But the bullet hole?

BARRISTER. What bullet hole?

JAMIE. *(Goes to where BARRISTER had pointed.)* Here. Right here in the wall where you saw it. Where is it?

BARRISTER. I said it was there. No one went and looked.

KAY. Then you're—

BARRISTER. Parker Madison, resume and photo on request from my agent.

KAY. You were brilliant.

JAMIE. I never guessed.

JOYCE. He plays my father in the show.

MILLICENT. I'm sorry about that coffee commercial. I mean I did it forty-three times that day we shot it and suddenly I just couldn't stop.

ALBERTINE. It all worked out, didn't it?

JAMIE. I'll have my development. *(Goes C.)*

KAY. *(her arms around him)* I'll have a husband.

ALBERTINE. Doris Durwood will get her recognition.

JOYCE. And just like a play everything ends happily.

ALBERTINE. No, dear, for a play to end there has to be one more surprise.

(PHONE rings.)

ALBERTINE. And this is probably it.

JAMIE. I thought the phone was dead.

BARRISTER. I just pretended.

JAMIE. Oh, *(into phone)* Durwood Enterprises ... Who? ...No ...

ALBERTINE. What is it?

JAMIE. It's the real H.L. Barrister. He's in town to discuss a mini-series.

ALBERTINE. That is a curtain line! *(They all chatter away as the CURTAIN FALLS.)*

PROPERTY LIST

ACT I:
SCENE 1:
Off Up Center:
3 cups of coffee (KAY)
Bottle of whiskey and glass (KAY)
Tea bag (KAY)

Off Right:
Small prescription bottle of pills (SPENCER)

On Stage:
Pen and pencils on desk
Phone book on desk
Typing paper in desk drawer
Small desk lamp upstage on desk

SCENE 2:
No change

ACT II:
Off Right:
2 large stuffed manila envelopes (SPENCER)
wallet (BARRISTER)
Revolver loaded with blanks (BUCK)

Off Up Center:
Tray with 4 coffee cups, cream and sugar, carafe of coffee on it. (KAY)
Glass of water and pill bottle with pills in it (MILLICENT.)

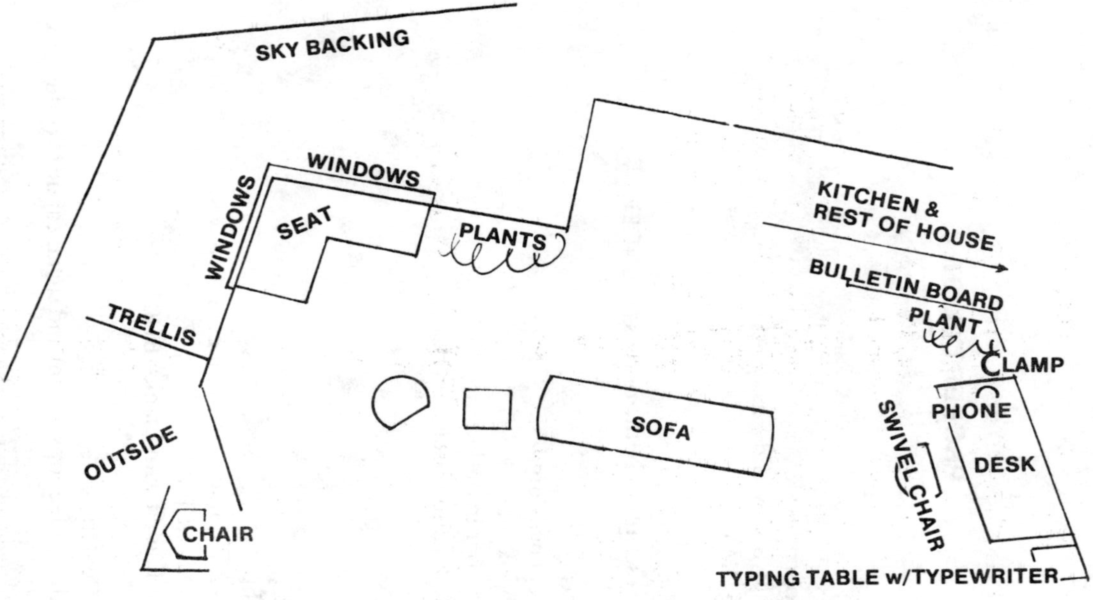

SCENE DESIGN
HOT PROPERTY

PROMENADE, ALL!

DAVID V. ROBISON

(Little Theatre) Comedy

3 Men, 1 Woman, Interior

Four actors play four successive generations of the same family, as their business grows from manufacturing buttons to a conglomerate of international proportions (in the U.S. their perfume will be called Belle Nuit; but in Paris, Enchanted Evening). The Broadway cast included Richard Backus, Anne Jackson, Eli Wallach and Hume Cronyn. Miss Jackson performed as either mother or grandmother, as called for; and Cronyn and Wallach alternated as fathers and grandfathers; with Backus playing all the roles of youth. There are some excellent cameos to perform, such as the puritanical mother reading the Bible to her son without realizing the sexual innuendoes; or the 90-year-old patriarch who is agreeable to trying an experiment in sexology but is afraid of a heart attack.

"So likeable; jolly and splendidly performed."—*N.Y. Daily News*. "The author has the ability to write amusing lines, and there are many of them."—*N.Y. Post*. "Gives strong, lively actors a chance for some healthy exercise. And what a time they have at it!"—*CBS-TV*.

ROYALTY, $50-$35

ACCOMMODATIONS

NICK HALL

(Little Theatre) Comedy

2 Men, 2 Women, Interior

Lee Schallert, housewife, feeling she may be missing out on something, leaves her husband, Bob, and her suburban home and moves into a two-room Greenwich Village apartment with two roommates. One roommate, Pat, is an aspiring actress, never out of characters or costumes, but, through an agency mix up, the other roommate is a serious, young, graduate student—male. The ensuing complications make a hysterical evening.

"An amusing study of marital and human relations . . . a gem . . . It ranks as one of the funniest ever staged."—*Labor Herald*. "The audience at Limestone Valley Dinner Theater laughed at "Accommodations" until it hurt."—*News American*. "Superior theater, frivolous, perhaps, but nonetheless superior. It is light comedy at its best."—*The Sun, Baltimore*.

ROYALTY, $50-$25

COUNT DRACULA

TED TILLER

(All Groups) Mystery comedy

7 Men, 2 Women. Interior with Small Inset

1930 Costumes (optional)

Based on Bram Stoker's 19th Century novel, "Dracula." This is a new, witty version of the classic story of a suave vampire whose passion is sinking his teeth into the throats of beautiful young women. Mina, his latest victim, is the ward of Dr. Seward in whose provincial insane asylum the terrifying action transpires. Her finance arrives from London, worried over her strange inertia and trance-like state. Equally concerned is Professor Van Helsing, specialist in rare maladies, who senses the supernatural at work. Added trouble comes from Sybil, Dr. Sewards demented, sherry-tippling sister and from Renfield, a schizophrenic inmate in league with the vampire. But how to trap this ghoul who can transform himself into a bat, materialize from fog, dissolve in mist? There are many surprising but uncomplicated stage effects, mysterious disappearances, secret panels, howling wolves, bats that fly over the audience, an unexpected murder, and magic tricks which include Dracula's vanishing in full view of the spectators.

Despite much gore, ". . . the play abounds with funny lines. There is nothing in it but entertainment."—*Springfield, Mass. News.*

ROYALTY, $50-$25

FRANKENSTEIN

TIM KELLY

(All Groups)

4 Men, 4 Women, Interior

Victor Frankenstein, a brilliant young scientist, returns to his chateau on the shores of Lake Geneva to escape some terrible pursuer. No one can shake free the dark secret that terrifies him. Not his mother, nor his financee Elizabeth, nor his best friend, Henry Clerval. Even the pleading of a gypsy girl accused of murdering Victor's younger brother falls on deaf ears, for Victor has brought into being a "Creature" made from bits and pieces of the dead! The Creature tracks Victor to his sanctuary to demand a bride to share its loneliness—one as wretched as the Creature itself. Against his better judgment, Victor agrees and soon the household is invaded by murder, despair and terror! The play opens on the wedding night of Victor and Elizabeth, the very time the Creature has sworn to kill the scientist for destroying its intended mate, and ends, weeks later, in a horrific climax of dramatic suspense! In between there is enough macabre humor to relieve the mounting tension. Perhaps the truest adaptation of Mary Shelley's classic yet. Simple to stage and a guaranteed audience pleaser.

ROYALTY, $25.00

Going Ape

NICK HALL

(Little Theatre.) Farce.

3 male, 2 female—Interior

This hilarious and almost indescribable farce has some serious undertones. Rupert, an idealistic and romantic young orphan, has come to his uncle's house to commit suicide. This proves to be no easy matter. For one thing he is constantly attended by his uncle's attractive nurse/secretary. He is also constantly interrupted by a stream of visitors, at first fairly normal, but increasingly incredible. Rupert realizes that all the visitors are the same three people, and his attention is drawn toward understanding the preposterously Victorian plot in which he is trapped, and which, in a startlingly theatrical climax, he begins to understand. "An intricate plot with subtle foreshadowing and a grab bag of surprises . . . some of the funniest characters you'll ever see molded into a tight dramatic package."—News, Fort Myers. "Every scene transcends not only the imagination, but melds into a literally death-defying whole. It's fast, like 2,000 mph . . . a play as old and as contemporary as today." Sarasota Journal. "Going Ape is truly zany . . . the wackiness is infectious." —Time.

(Royalty, $50-$25.)

Eat Your Heart Out

NICK HALL

(Little Theatre.) Comedy.

3 male, 2 female—Interior

In this theatrical comedy Charlie, an out of work actor currently employed as a waiter, takes the audience through a sequence of hilarious encounters in a succession of Manhattan restaurants. By changing the tablecloths during the course of the action the basic setting of three tables and six chairs becomes a variety of New York restaurants, both elegant and shabby. The scenes change, the action is uninterrupted and the comedy never stops. The other performers play several parts: the girl desperately trying to eat snails and oysters to please her fiance; the middle-aged couple whose marriage is breaking up; the lovers so intent on each other they cannot order dinner; the rich, embittered astrologer; the timid man who never gets a waiter; the agents, directors, actors, and waiters. An amusing gallery of characters whose stories intertwine and finally involve Charlie. The author of "Accommodations" has written a very funny, contemporary play that is also a serious comedy of backstage life. ". . . a sharp, stunning play. It'll make you howl—but better yet, it might even make you sniffle a bit."—Fort Lauderdale News. "Tightly written and very, very entertaining. I recommend it enthusiastically."—Miami Herald. ". . . About as good as anything I've ever seen in dinner theater . . ."—Fort Lauderdale Times.

(Royalty, $50-$25.)

HERE'S HOW

A Basic Stagecraft Book

THOROUGHLY REVISED AND ENLARGED

by HERBERT V. HAKE

COVERING 59 topics on the essentials of stagecraft (13 of them brand new). *Here's How* meets a very real need in the educational theater. It gives to directors and others concerned with the technical aspects of play production a complete and graphic explanation of ways of handling fundamental stagecraft problems.

The book is exceptional on several counts. It not only treats every topic thoroughly, but does so in an easy-to-read style every layman can understand. Most important, it is prepared in such a way that for every topic there is a facing page of illustrations (original drawings and photographs)—thus giving the reader a complete graphic presentation of the topic along with the textual description of the topic.

Because of the large type, the large size of the pages (9″ x 12″), and the flexible metal binding, *Here's How* will lie flat when opened and can be laid on a workbench for a director to read while in a *standing* position.

HOME-BUILT

Lighting Equipment

for The Small Stage

By THEODORE FUCHS

This volume presents a series of fourteen simplified designs for building various types of stage lighting and control equipment, with but one purpose in mind—to enable the amateur producer to acquire a complete set of stage lighting equipment at the lowest possible cost. The volume is 8½" x 11" in size, with heavy paper and spiral binding—features which make the volume well suited to practical workshop use.

Community Theatre

A MANUAL FOR SUCCESS

By JOHN WRAY YOUNG

The ideal text for anyone interested in participating in Community Theatre as a vocation or avocation. "Organizing a Community Theatre," "A Flight Plan for the Early Years," "Programming for People—Not Computers," and other chapters are blueprints for solid growth. "Technical, Business and Legal Procedures" cuts a safe and solvent path through some tricky undergrowth. Essential to the library of all community theatres, and to the schools who will supply them with talent in the years to come.

SAMUEL FRENCH has:

AMERICA'S FAVORITE COMEDIES

ABSURD PERSON SINGULAR – ACCOMMODATIONS – ANGEL ON MY SHOULDER – BAREFOOT IN THE PARK – A BEDFULL OF FOREIGNERS – BEDROOM FARCE – BUTTERFLIES ARE FREE – CACTUS FLOWER – CALIFORNIA SUITE – CHAMPAGNE COMPLEX – CHAPTER TWO – CHARLIE'S AUNT – A COUPLA WHITE CHICKS – DON'T DRINK THE WATER – THE DREAM CRUST – FLING! – FOOLS – THE FOURPOSTER – THE GIN GAME – THE GINGERBREAD LADY – GOD'S FAVORITE THE GOOD DOCTOR – HERE LIES JEREMY TROY – I OUGHT TO BE IN PICTURES – THE IMPOSSIBLE YEARS – IN ONE BED . . . AND OUT THE OTHER – IT HAD TO BE YOU – KINDLING – THE LADY WHO CRIED FOX – LOVE, SEX AND THE I.R.S. – LOVERS AND OTHER STRANGERS – LUNCH HOUR – THE MARRIAGE-GO-ROUND

For descriptions of plays, consult our Basic Catalogue of Plays.